HIGHER
BUSINESS
MANAGEMENT

HOW TO PASS

HIGHER
BUSINESS
MANAGEMENT

Peter Hagan

Hodder Gibson

A MEMBER OF THE HODDER HEADLINE GROUP

Acknowledgements

Cartoons © Moira Munro 2005

Every effort has been made to trace all copyright holders, but if any have been inadvertently overlooked the Publishers will be pleased to make the necessary arrangements at the first opportunity.

Although every effort has been made to ensure that website addresses are correct at time of going to press, Hodder Gibson cannot be held responsible for the content of any website mentioned in this book. It is sometimes possible to find a relocated web page by typing in the address of the home page for a website in the URL window of your browser.

Papers used in this book are natural, renewable and recyclable products. They are made from wood grown in sustainable forests. The logging and manufacturing processes conform to the environmental regulations of the country of origin.

Orders: please contact Bookpoint Ltd, 130 Milton Park, Abingdon, Oxon OX14 4SB. Telephone: (44) 01235 827720. Fax: (44) 01235 400454. Lines are open from 9.00 – 6.00, Monday to Saturday, with a 24 hour message answering service. Visit our website at www.hoddereducation.co.uk. Hodder Gibson can be contacted direct on: Tel: 0141 848 1609; Fax: 0141 889 6315; email: hoddergibson@hodder.co.uk

© Peter Hagan 2005
First published in 2005 by
Hodder Gibson, a member of the Hodder Headline Group
2a Christie Street
Paisley PA1 1NB

Impression number 10 9 8 7 6 5 4 3 2
Year 2010 2009 2008 2007 2006 2005

Cover photo © Photodisc Blue (E011013)
Typeset in 9.5pt Frutiger Light by Dorchester Typesetting Group Ltd
Printed and bound in Great Britain by Martins The Printer, Berwick-upon-Tweed

A catalogue record for this title is available from the British Library

ISBN 10: 0 340 885564

ISBN 13: 9780 340 885567

CONTENTS

AN INTRODUCTION TO HIGHER BUSINESS MANAGEMENT

Welcome To This Revision Book

Congratulations! You have just taken the first step in passing and improving the grade you get in your final exam.

By buying this guide you have shown that you are taking your exams seriously, which is good. However, it is not a textbook and it does not contain the whole course. This is what it does include.

◆ A summary of the course.

◆ Study and revision hints.

◆ Examination techniques for success.

◆ Practice questions and answers for the final exam.

◆ What you need to know for the internal assessments

So, How Do You Pass Higher Business Management?

The answer should be work hard, study well and you will pass. However, like all things in life, it is never that simple. Even if you do pass, will you get the grade you should?

Remember

Here are some points to remember.

◆ The difference between a pass and a fail in the exam is only one mark.

◆ The difference between an A and a B grade, and between a B and a C, is only one mark.

◆ There are only 11 marks between an A grade and a C.

The job of this guide is to help you get those extra marks that will make sure you not only pass, but get the highest grade you can.

Should it not be my teacher that makes this happen?

The short answer is yes. However, the long answer is that even the very best teachers cannot get every student in their class the best possible grade.

How Will This Guide Help?

Summary

There are two units in Higher Business Management. These are divided into eight sections.

Unit 1: Business enterprise
Section 1: Business in contemporary society
Section 2: Business Information ICT
Section 3: Decision-making in business

Unit 2: Business decision areas
Section 1: Internal organisation
Section 2: Marketing
Section 3: Financial management
Section 4: Human resources management
Section 5: Operations management

Internal assessments

You have to pass the internal assessments for both of the units to get the full course award, so these are important. With a little preparation, passing them is straightforward, and the guide gives hints on how to do this.

The exam

The guide covers some important exam techniques to help you tackle the paper, and then explains what the markers are looking for. This may be a bit different from what your teacher or lecturer has told you, but there is no need to worry.

Some exam type questions are given, and the book shows you how they are marked.

Course content

The guide also explains what should be included in the course. The problem here is that the core notes do not include everything they should, and neither do most revision guides.

Study And Revision Techniques

How can you learn it all!

Breaking the work into sections

The course is broken down into topics, so rather than try to learn everything at once, work on each topic in turn.

Lists and bullet points

Use bullet points to make short summaries of the relevant pieces of information for each topic.

Here is a list of short-term pricing strategies.

Example

♦ Skimming.

♦ Penetration pricing.

♦ Destroyer pricing.

♦ Promotional pricing.

♦ Demand-orientated pricing.

Learn the list, and then practise writing explanations for each.

List and bullet points are much easier to remember than whole explanations, and are easier to use in the exam.

Throughout the course there are lists of advantages and disadvantages which can be easily learned, and are common answers in the exam. Try making these into lists to memorise.

Making your memory work

Remembering facts is not as hard as it first appears.

The problem that most students have is in moving information from their short-term memory to their long-term memory. There are a number of ways to do this, but the most effective is repetition, doing the same thing over and over again. Sorry, but it is true! Your brain is like a muscle. The more you use it, the more effective it is.

Another good technique is to teach your brain to organise facts together. What you have learned in class needs to be organised in your brain so you can remember it when you need to.

You may be surprised to learn that one of the best ways to do this is to organise the work you have done in class on paper. Organise your notes and folders, use dividers, use your diary, rewrite your notes in words you can understand, or even key them into a computer. Do all this from the start of your course!

Learning styles

We are all different, so what works for other people may not work for you. You can find out what your own learning style is on the Internet by going to www.bbc.co.uk/keyskills and clicking on 'Extras'.

You can use this information to help you draw up a study plan and decide what revision techniques to use. Remember though that there is no better way to learn than by doing the same thing over and over again.

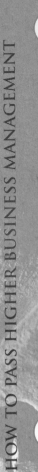

General Examination Techniques

Language

In business, communication has to be effective. The person receiving the communication needs to be able to understand easily what they have to do. Therefore the language of the communication should be simple and straightforward.

It is the same for your answers in Higher Business Management examinations. Do not make them over-complicated, and say exactly what you mean to say, in the simplest form you can.

No extra marks are given for elaborate prose, and indeed students often lose marks because they have ended up not giving the answer that was wanted. It is sometimes obvious to the marker what the student intended to say, but if they do not actually say it, then the mark cannot be given.

Keep your language simple.

Imagine that the marker is a complete idiot who understands nothing about business management. Then you should end up explaining carefully what you mean and getting the marks.

What to write

There are two things which make the marker's job more difficult. The first is having to read through pages and pages of a student's script before they get to the bit where the student starts to answer the question.

A student might decide that the best way to answer a question was to rewrite the question, then write a few paragraphs on any words that appeared in the question, then write a brief description of the answer they were going to give, then answer the question, and finally provide a summary of their answer to the question.

It is possible that this student would get good marks for their answer, but they would be likely to run out of time at the end of the exam. There are also plenty of answers where the student gets all their marks for their introduction, and the rest of the answer is just repetition.

Time is precious in the exam, so use it well.

If you think this sounds as if you should write less in you are answers, then you are wrong. The more you write, the better the chance you have of getting more marks (remember that there is only one mark between a pass and a fail).

It is how much you write that is important. No marks are taken off for wrong answers, so it does not matter if part of your answer is wrong,

Many students will not write answers they are unsure about, in case they look stupid. This is the last thing you should worry about. Markers do not look at the names of candidates or which school they are from while they are marking. Even if they did, they would have no idea who you were. They are only concerned with giving you all the marks you deserve.

Write as much as you can, even if you are not 100 per cent sure that you are correct. Just do not repeat yourself.

Handwriting

The second problem that markers have is bad handwriting. Some candidates with very poor handwriting are allowed to use a computer to key in their answers, or they have someone to write their answers for them. If necessary, check with your school to see if this would apply to you.

If it would not, and your handwriting is poor, you should look at ways of improving it. A little time spent on this now will help in all your exams.

Check to see if other people can read your handwriting easily. Even if writing is very neat, it is sometimes difficult to read. If this is a problem, try printing your letters rather than joining them up.

Remember that you need to communicate with the marker. Make sure that your handwriting is easy to understand so that you do not lose marks in the exam.

If you are running out of time at the end of the exam, watch that your writing does not get worse.

The Question Paper: Section One

The Higher Business Management paper is split into two parts, with 50 marks being available for each part. The first part, Section One, is often called 'the case study', although it is actually a piece of what is called 'stimulus material'. All the questions in Section One *must* be answered

Question 1

The only question that is actually about the stimulus material is Question 1, and it is worth ten marks.

It asks you to identify and sometimes analyse the problems faced by a business. For most students this presents a number of challenges. These are some of the problems.

Common Mistakes

- ◆ Students cannot identify the business's problems.
- ◆ Students offer solutions. Writing about what the business should do is not asked for, and will not get you any marks. So do not do it!
- ◆ Students put the problems under the wrong headings. It can sometimes be difficult to decide which headings they should appear under.
- ◆ Students do not put in any headings at all.

Thus even if you can identify ten problems, you can still end up with low marks for the question.

Those extra few marks can mean the difference between a pass and a fail, an A and a B, and so on. Let us examine how you can get all the marks available for this question.

Identifying problems

A problem is anything that means the business has to take some action. This can be because good things are happening or bad things are happening.

Offering solutions

Example

In the question in the 2003 paper, the business was too successful and had to turn away orders. Was this a problem?

Many students thought it was a marketing problem. However, there was no mention of any marketing strategy in the question. Others thought it was a financial problem, but the company had been successful in obtaining additional finance. Some assumed that it was a human resources problem, and others listed it under 'other problems'. Quite a large number of students wrote about what they thought the company should do about it. *None of these students received any marks*. Why not?

Example continued ➤

Example *continued*

All successful companies have to turn away work from time to time, so this would not in itself have been a problem. However, if you could link the situation to something else, then you could earn marks.

- 'They had to turn work away because they did not have sufficient resources to diversify', [It was a human resources problem.]
- 'They had to turn work away that would go to competitors, which could lead to them losing further work to competitors in the future.' [It was a marketing problem.]

Either of these answers would have received a mark.

Suggesting what the company should have done or should do in the future is a waste of time. Do not do it.

Which heading?

This problem is easily solved. If you do not know which heading to put a problem under, put it under more than one! No marks are taken off for doing this so you have nothing to lose.

The only drawback to this is shortage of time. Some students have been known to put all the problems under all the headings; they do well in Question 1, but run out of time at the end.

No headings

If you do not follow the instructions in the question and put the headings in, the markers are under instructions to treat your whole answer as being under one heading, which means you are unlikely to get more than three marks. So always put in the headings!

The other questions

The rest of Section One contains questions that refer to the 'case study', but none of the answers are in it. You will need to rely on what you have learned from your previous studies to answer these questions. However, there are a couple of techniques that can help.

Check the allocated marks

Look at the number of marks allocated to each part of each question. This will tell you how much you need to write.

Example

'How might the Internet prove to be a useful tool for a business trying to expand outside its home market?   2 marks'

Only two marks are available for this question, so you would only need to make a couple of points (perhaps three to play safe).

Read the question

Read the question carefully to make sure you understand what you are being asked.

Example

Look at the question in the example above. It does not ask how a business can use the Internet to expand, but how it can expand abroad (outside its home market). Therefore your answers would have to be related to and mention consumers in other countries who use the Internet.

◆ 'Customers can purchase goods on the Internet.' [This would probably not earn any marks.]

◆ 'The company could develop a website where customers around the world could view its products.' [This would receive a mark.]

◆ 'Customers abroad could log onto the website and purchase goods using a credit card.' [This would also receive a mark.]

Another example

Example

'The business has implemented a new staff appraisal programme. How might a business assess the effectiveness of any staff appraisal programme? 4 marks'

Here the question appears to ask about staff appraisal, but it does not. The question is about the evaluation of the programme, and evaluation methods are similar for most aspects of the business. How good was it? How can we measure how good it was?

Four marks are available for this question so you need to make at least four points.

You should apply some common sense. If you wanted to know how good a film was, how would you find out? Ask someone who had seen it!

Example continued ➤

Example continued

The following answers would all earn marks.

◆ 'Ask staff how they feel the appraisal system worked for them.'

◆ 'Find out if staff were more motivated or less motivated after the appraisal.'

◆ 'Measure staff productivity to see if the staff are now more productive.'

◆ 'Ask staff if they feel that the targets set are reasonable.'

Summary

◆ Look at the marks that are available for each question, and make your answers match the marks available.

◆ Look closely at what the question is asking. This is a common cause of students not getting the marks that their knowledge should earn for them.

The Question Paper:

Section Two of the paper is often referred to as 'the essay questions', but they are not really essay questions.

You have to choose two questions out of five in this section.

Both Section One and Section Two are designed to test you on as many parts of the course as possible. However, in Section Two, the questions are more likely to test you on straightforward knowledge and understanding, and there will usually be more marks available for each part of the questions than for those in Section One.

There are a couple of useful techniques that you can use to make sure you get the most marks you can.

Choose the right questions

Remember

◆ Read each part of each question carefully so you know exactly what you are being asked to write about.

◆ Look at the marks that are available for each part of each question.

Key words

A number of key words are included in the questions. They give you guidance on what you are expected to do.

Key Words

★ **Advantages and disadvantages**

This term asks you to look at the possible benefits and drawbacks of options. Be careful how you answer these questions. You will not usually get marks if you state an advantage and then use exactly the opposite of it for a disadvantage. (For example, if you were asked to give the advantages and disadvantages of introducing a new marketing campaign, you might not get marks for a disadvantage if you said that an advantage would be increased consumer awareness while a disadvantage of not introducing it would be lost consumer awareness.

★ **Compare and contrast**

This asks you to look at two or more options and identify the similarities and differences. (For example, if you were asked to compare and contrast sole traders and private limited companies, then your answer should look something like this. 'A sole tradership is a business owned by one individual, whereas a private limited company is owned by a group of shareholders …'

★ **Define**

This indicates that the examiner is usually looking for an explanation of a business term. Although one is not always asked for, an example will help to make sure you get the marks, as it will show that you really do know what you are writing about.

★ **Describe**

This is similar to 'define' in terms of what the examiner is looking for in your answer. However, there tends to be more to write about in 'describe' questions, and therefore more marks are available for them.

★ **Explain**

This term is very similar to 'define' and 'describe', and again examples will help your answer, whether they are asked for or not.

★ **Identify**

There are very few marks for 'identifying', as they are easy to get. You are usually asked for a straightforward name or names. (For example, you may be asked to identify sources of finance for a business.)

Key Words continued ➤

Key Words *continued*

★ **Identify and describe**

The examiner is asking you to name something and then give an explanation of why you have named it. (In the example above of identifying sources of finance, your answer could be as follows. 'Bank loan: A set amount of money borrowed from the bank for a particular purpose.

★ **Justify**

This asks you to give good reasons for a decision. (In the bank loan example, you could write the following. 'You receive the money fairly quickly and can pay it back over a period of time, so large amounts of money can be obtained and the repayment can be planned over a number of years.')

★ **Outline**

This asks you to summarise a 'description' without giving too much detail.

Choosing the right questions is vital

Some parts of the course will be very fresh in your memory, and you will be tempted to pick questions that ask you about these areas.

However, before you jump in, look at the numbers of marks available, and decide how many marks you think you could get. Then look at the other parts of the question and see how many marks you could get there. There is no point in tackling a question where you are guaranteed five marks because you know that topic well, only to find that the other parts of the question do not suit you at all.

Success in this part of the paper comes through reading all the questions carefully and working out which will get you the most marks. You do have a choice, so make it work for you!

Using bullet points

The use of bullet points is a common business method for making information more readable, summarising information, and saving time. You are studying business management, so use them!

The main problem with bullet points is understanding the difference between bullet points and a list. A bullet point is a sentence. It may be short, but it should contain a verb. A list, on the other hand, is just a series of brief headings.

Example

'Describe the stages which take place before a product reaches the market. 8 marks'

You can use bullet points to answer this question. (Like many questions, it asks you to 'describe', so a simple list will not gain many marks.)

This is how to answer the quesion in bullet points.

These are the stages a product will go through before it reaches the market.

◆ Generate the idea, through market research or brainstorming.

◆ Analyse the idea. Can the business produce it? Will it sell? Can enough profit be made? Does it comply with legal standards?

◆ Create a prototype or mock-up of the product to see what it would look like.

◆ Ask a consumer panel and carry out market research to get the opinions of potential customers.

◆ Make any changes that are needed as a result of the consumers' comments.

◆ Arrange for the product to be patented etc. to make sure that no one can steal the idea.

◆ Decide on a price for the product that will allow the business to make the profit level it wants.

◆ Arrange or find the finance necessary to produce and launch the product.

Example continued ➤

Example continued

♦ Carry out the necessary promotional activities to make sure the launch is a success.

♦ Launch the product onto the whole market or a test market.

The above answer should get full marks, and will take up less than a page. To write this as full paragraphs would take a lot longer.

This is how the question might be answered with a list.

♦ Get idea.

♦ Analyse idea.

♦ Make a prototype.

♦ Test the prototype.

♦ Make changes.

♦ Obtain patents.

♦ Work out a price.

♦ Find finance for the launch.

♦ Advertise.

♦ Launch the product.

This answer would earn you few if any marks. Although both of the answers show that the student knows the answer to the question, the list does not 'describe', as was asked for in the question.

Summary

♦ Read the questions carefully so you understand exactly what is being asked.

♦ Work out which questions will get you the most marks.

♦ Use bullet points where you can to give yourself more time and more chance of getting marks.

Problem Questions

Getting the mixes mixed up

Most students know about the marketing mix. This can cause a problem: when they see the word 'mix' they start to write about the marketing mix.

There are two other mixes in the course: the 'product mix' and the 'purchasing mix'. These are completely different from the marketing mix, so make sure you know which one you are being asked about.

The **product mix** is the range of products that an organisation offers for sale. Questions about the product mix will be looking for answers about what makes a good product mix.

♦ Products at different stages in the life cycle.

♦ Products which use the same basic raw materials.

♦ Products which are delivered to the same retailers.

♦ Products that appeal to a variety of market segments.

The **purchasing mix** is what an organisation's purchasing department has to think about when buying materials.

- Alternative suppliers.
- Delivery times.
- Price.
- Quality.
- Quality.
- Storage facilities.

Diagrams

Some questions may ask for diagrams. In others, the use of diagrams will gain marks. For example, questions on the product life cycle, the product portfolio and stock control will all allow you to draw a diagram to help you to gain full marks. The Boston matrix is also acceptable (although it is not actually correct).

One potential problem is that the diagrams have to be complete and accurate. The axes should be properly labelled, and nothing should be missed out. Missing out information will mean that it will be unlikely that you will get any marks for your diagram.

The other problem is that diagrams take time to draw, but you are only likely to get one or two marks for them. Therefore you have to decide whether they are worth the time they take.

As a rule, draw diagrams if you are asked to. They do not have to be works of art, so do not worry about being too neat, but make sure you miss nothing out!

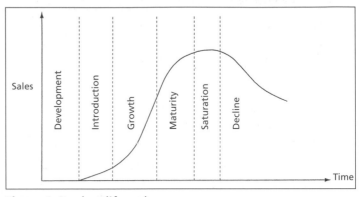

Figure 1 Product life cycle

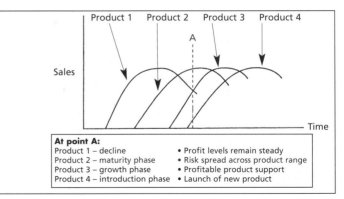

Figure 2 Product portfolio

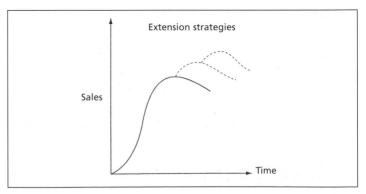

Figure 3 Life-cycle extension strategies

If you are not asked for a diagram, one can still be useful to show that you know what you are writing about, and it can get you additional marks. However, you must make sure that it is complete.

Public relations

Questions about the role of public relations officers have been popular in recent years, but very few students get full marks for them. This is because they often misunderstand the role.

Although public relations officers are included under marketing, they are not directly involved in it. Their function is to deal with corporate communications between the company and consumers, government and pressure groups. They do not really get involved in marketing communications.

They organise press releases and make charitable donations, and participate in the organisation's corporate social responsibility programmes, event sponsorship and celebrity endorsements. They may also be involved with customer services in some organisations.

Types of decision

This is a hard one! (Even teachers can get this wrong sometimes.) The main thing to remember is that **strategic decisions** are about setting objectives or targets for the organisation. **Tactical decisions** are mainly about how to achieve those targets and put resources into place. **Operational decisions** are made in response to changes in the internal and external working environment.

Example

- ◆ Cadbury decides to strengthen and unite its brand image. This is a strategic decision.
- ◆ Some existing products in the range are given new packaging. For example, the *Caramel* logo is made smaller, and the *Dairy Milk* logo is made bigger. This is a tactical decision.
- ◆ Details of the new packaging are sent to suppliers. This is an operational decision.

Channels of distribution

The channel of distribution is not about the types of transportation that are available to a business when taking its goods to market. These questions look at whether the organisation should use wholesalers, agents and retailers, and what type of retail outlet would best suit the product.

The answers should be based around the following.

◆ Nature of the product: For example is it perishable? Is specialist advice required.

◆ Size of market: For example if it is a small market, then sell directly. If it is a large, widespread market, then use retailers.

◆ Location of market: For example in a global market, local agents may be required.

◆ Legal requirements: For example alcohol and drugs can only be sold through approved outlets.

CORPORATE CULTURE

Definition:

> **"The values, beliefs and norms relating to the organisation that are shared by all staff."**

So what does that mean?

People in organisations behave in a similar manner. The way they act towards each other, how they deal with customers and others outside the organisation, how they dress, how they approach their work, etc. They become part of the social group of workers within that organisation.

Managers can set their own corporate culture as a method of influencing the way staff behave in the workplace. This can be as simple as a list of rules, or a set of policies adopted by the organisation.

This can be particularly useful when the organisation is spread throughout various locations across the country or even the world. It will influence what staff feel to be important, what they accept as normal practise, and so how they act at work. This will bring them together as a group.

The **advantages** of a corporate culture would be:

◆ Employees will feel part of the organisation,

◆ Staff will have increased motivation and job satisfaction,

◆ Team work will improve with better employee relationships,

◆ Staff will be more loyal to the organisation, with lower staff turnover,

◆ Motivated workers produce more, and of a better quality,

◆ They will have shared goals, with the aims and objectives of the organisation carried, throughout all branches of the organisation.

The **drawbacks** of a corporate culture would be:

◆ It may stifle creative thinking,

◆ Some essential staff would find it difficult to fit in,

◆ Time and effort are required to maintain the culture and for new staff to adapt to the culture,

◆ Change may be more difficult to implement.

Quota and Random Sampling

Students often have difficulty confusing 'quota' and 'random' sampling. The problem lies with the names of each type.

Quota sampling

Here the market researchers are given a number of different types of consumer. For example, they may be asked to interview 20 females between the ages of 15 and 20, and 20 females between the ages of 20 and 25. They then have to find 20 females in each age group and interview them.

They just pick the first 20 people that fit into each age group and then stop.

It is quicker and cheaper than random sampling as they don't have to interview named people.

Random sampling

Here the people to be interviewed are selected at random from a data source such as the telephone book. Once a person had been selected the researcher has to interview that actual person, and they are not normally allowed to substitute them with someone else.

They have to wait to find them at home, and can speak to them only when they are willing to be interviewed. This makes life more difficult for the researcher and can take up a lot of time and effort.

So in quota sampling the person who actually answers the interviewers questions can be just a '**random**' off the street as long as they fit the correct characteristics of the person to be interviewed. Where as, in random sampling once a person has been selected, you have to interview them.

Other problems

Some questions will ask you about things which have not been covered in the course. This is because you are expected to have a good rounded knowledge of the business world.

This is always changing, and some parts of the course are now becoming a bit dated. For example it still covers total quality management, when firms these days are more concerned with lean production.

Reading quality newspapers and watching the news will give you a much better appreciation of the business world. There are also some useful websites.

◆ www.times100.co.uk

◆ www.bbc.co.uk
(Search for Working Lunch, and then click on 'Lunch Lessons'.)

◆ www.bized.ac.uk

Each of these provides short, entertaining, up-to-date case studies that will significantly enhance your knowledge.

Development marks

A development point is where a student has answered the question, but then goes on to develop the answer by adding more to show that they have a good understanding of the topic they are being asked about.

A question often asked is 'Are there any marks available for development points?'. The answer is yes, however, they are not available in all questions in the paper.

Unfortunately, it is not always obvious where development marks will be given. As a rough guide, the more marks there are for a question, the more likely development marks are available. So, if a question is worth two marks then it is unlikely that there is any opportunity to gain additional development marks, whereas if it is worth 5 marks or more then it is more likely development marks will be available.

Should you try to make development points?

The answer is a definite YES!

Just as your use of examples helps the examiner make up their mind that you have indeed answered the question and deserve the mark, developing the answer will help you make sure you get the marks you should. Although many students simply say the same thing again in a different way it often helps to ensure that they get the mark. There are no marks available for repeating, but trying to explain the point better will make sure you get the mark.

Look at the examples of answers given below.

Question: Describe the advantages of a decentralised structure to the organisation.

◆ Example of an undeveloped answer:

'Managers will be more motivated in a decentralised structure.'

This answer may well not get a mark. It shows the student knows what an advantage of the decentralised structure is, but the student does not describe it.

◆ Example of a developed answer:

'Because managers further down the chain of command will be allowed to make some of their own decisions, they will be more motivated.'

Here the student will get the mark because there has been some description of the point that managers will be more motivated.

◆ Example of a well developed answer with development points:

'A decentralised structure allows decision-making to be passed down the structure to middle and lower managers, this will increase their motivation.   (1 mark)

More motivated managers can be more effective in the quality and quantity of their output, (1 mark) and are likely to be more effective in the motivation of their subordinates.   (1 mark)'

Here the student **may** get up to three marks. The answer not only shows that the student knows and can describe the fact that a decentralised structure will motivate managers, but has gone on to describe the benefits of that motivation.

Summary
Development marks are available in many of the questions in the paper, so try and get some. Trying to develop your answers will increase the chances of getting full marks for a question.

PART 1

Business Enterprise

BUSINESS ENTERPRISE: BUSINESS IN CONTEMPORARY SOCIETY

What You Should Know

The role of business in society	Business activity. Durable goods. Non-durable goods. Services. Factors of production: land, labour, capital and enterprise. Wealth creation. Cycle of business. Sectors of industrial activity: primary, secondary and tertiary. De-industrialisation.
Types of business organisation	Private sector: sole traders, partnerships, private and public limited companies, and franchises. Public sector: public corporations, government-funded service providers, and local authorities.
The role of the entrepreneur	Functions and importance of entrepreneurs.
Factors affecting the operation of the business	Socio-cultural factors, technological factors and economic factors. Sources of finance. Methods of growth. Competitive environment.
Business objectives	Survival, growth and development, profit maximisation, social responsibility, provision of products and services, etc.
Stakeholders	Identification of stakeholders, and how stakeholder relationships can affect the business.

Example

SAQ 1   a)   What is business activity?

b)   Describe the two different classifications of goods.

c)   Describe the factors of production.

d)   Why is wealth creation important to our society?

e)   What are the sectors of industrial activity?

Answer to SAQ 1

a)   This is any activity that provides us with goods and services to satisfy our wants. The **output** of business activity is the goods and services that we want.

b)   ◆   **Durable goods:** We can use these again and again. Examples are computers and CD players.

◆   **Non-durable goods:** Non-durable goods are things that we can normally only use once, such as food, drinks and newspapers.

c)   These are the resources that businesses need to produce goods and services.

◆   **Land**: This includes all the natural resources, such as oil, water and the land itself.

◆   **Labour**: This comprises the physical and mental efforts of workers.

◆   **Capital**: This consists of all the man-made resources.

◆   **Enterprise**: Enterprise is the human effort and will to provide goods and services. The entrepreneur is the person who brings together all the other resources and takes the risks to produce the goods or services.

d)   The more business activity there is, and the more goods and services are produced, the wealthier a country is. Thus the more we produce, the better off we can become.

e)   ◆   **Primary sector**: This consists of the business involved in exploiting or extracting natural resources (for example farming, mining, fishing and oil exploration).

◆   **Secondary sector**: These are the businesses that are involved in manufacturing and construction (for example car manufacturers and building firms).

◆   **Tertiary (service) sector**: This comprises the business that provide services rather than goods (for example banking and tourism).

Example continued ➤

Example

SAQ 2   a)   Describe the different types of private business organisation and the advantages and disadvantages of each.

b)   Discuss the role of the voluntary sector in business.

c)   Describe the different types of organisation operating in the public sector.

Answer to SAQ 2

a)   **A sole tradership** is a business that is owned and managed by one person. (Examples are small shops, hairdressers and tradespeople.)

Advantages

◆   They are very simple to set up.

◆   You get to make all the decisions.

◆   You get to keep all the profits

Disadvantages

◆   Borrowing from banks can be more difficult.

◆   A sole trader has unlimited liability.

◆   He or she has to run the business without help.

A partnership is a type of business that is owned and controlled by between two and 20 people (except for solicitors' and accountancy firms, which are allowed more).

Advantages

◆   The partners can share the responsibilities of running the firm.

◆   Partners can specialise (for instance one could be a plumber and another an electrician).

◆   More money is available to be invested in the business because there are more owners.

Disadvantages

◆   The partners have unlimited liability (except for certain types of sleeping partner).

◆   There may be arguments between the partners about how to run the business.

◆   Partners can leave and new partners can be taken on, which can upset the running of the business.

There are two types of limited company.

◆   Public limited companies (which have 'Plc' at the end of their name).

◆   Private limited companies (which have 'Ltd' at the end of their name).

Example continued ➤

Example *continued*

To create a limited company in the UK, you must register the company with the Registrar of Companies and complete two legal documents, the Memorandum of Association and the Articles of Association. These set out the aims of the business and how it will be run and financed. The main difference between the two types of company is that public limited companies are allowed to sell their shares to the public through the stock exchange.

Advantages

- The shareholders have limited liability.
- Private limited companies do not have to disclose most of the information that public limited companies have to provide to the public, such as their annual reports.
- Public limited companies can buy and sell their shares at any time and raise capital in this way. This means that they find it easier to plan, develop and expand.

Disadvantages

- All companies must be registered with the Registrar of Companies.
- Large organisations can be very difficult to manage properly or well, because of diseconomies of scale.
- It is more difficult to keep workers happy and well motivated in a big organisation.
- Setting up and administrating the legal requirements placed on limited companies generates costs.

Franchises are business arrangements in which one firm (the franchisee) pays for the right to trade under the name of another (the franchiser).

Advantages

- The franchiser can expand without having to buy additional premises or recruit, train and pay staff.

- The franchisee gets the franchiser's well established name and reputation and brand products.

- The franchisee is helped and supported by the franchiser, including benefiting from its advertising and its established quality processes.

- Product innovation can be shared among all the franchisees.

Example *continued* ➤

Example continued

Disadvantages

◆ The reputation of the franchise depends upon how good the franchisees are. If there is one piece of bad publicity about a single product or branch, it affects all the branches.

◆ The franchise agreement allows the franchiser to tell the franchisee exactly how to run the business. The franchisee may have to buy all its supplies from the franchiser.

◆ The franchisee has to pay part of its profits or a percentage of its sales revenue to the franchiser.

b) The main aim of organisations in the **voluntary sector** is not to make profits, but to raise money for good causes, or to provide services to the public which would otherwise not be provided, or not be provided well. In the UK, charities have to be registered with the Charity Commissioners, who watch over their activities. To be recognised as a charity, an organisation has to have one or more of the following as its main objective(s).

◆ To relieve poverty.

◆ To advance education.

◆ To advance religion.

◆ To carry out activities beneficial to the community.

c) **Public sector organisations** are set up and owned by a government to provide services to the public.

◆ **Public corporations** are businesses that are owned and run by the government for the people. Examples in the UK are the BBC and currently the Royal Mail. The Government appoints a chairperson and board of directors to run the business on its behalf.

◆ **Government-funded service providers** are responsible in the UK for services such as the National Health Service, Social Security, and Defence. They are financed by the Government to carry out the Government's policies in these areas. Each year, they are given a specific amount of money to spend.

◆ **Local authorities** in the UK provide the public with services such as education, housing, leisure and recreation, and street lighting. They get their income from council tax, government grants, and fees (for example from people using facilities at sports centres).

Example

SAQ 3   a)   Why is the entrepreneur so important for our society?

Answer to SAQ 3

a)   The **entrepreneur** is the individual or group who combines the factors of production to produce goods or services. If someone did not take on the role of the entrepreneur, nothing would be produced. They identify an opportunity to provide new goods or services, or to provide existing goods or services more cheaply or in a better way. They use their own money or borrowed money to put all the necessary resources together. They are usually risk takers, standing to lose everything if the idea does not work.

Example

SAQ 4   a)   Outline the external influences on business activity.

         b)   Identify the sources of long-term and short-term finance for organisations.

         c)   Outline the methods of growth available to organisations.

         d)   Identify the internal pressures for change in an organisation.

Answer to SAQ 4

a)
- ◆ **Socio-cultural influences**: changes in tastes, fashions and demographics.
- ◆ **Technological influences:** the introduction of new technologies (for example in advertising and selling on the Internet).
- ◆ **Economic influences**: changes in interest rates and exchange rates, and booms and slumps in the economy.
- ◆ **Political influences**: changes in legislation (for example on health and safety), competition, employment, etc.

Example continued ➢

Example *continued*

- ◆ **Competitive influences**: new products launched by competitors, changes in prices, advertising, etc.

b)
- ◆ Long-term: banks, grants, the selling of shares or debentures, leasing, mortgages, retained profits, and the selling of unwanted assets.
- ◆ Short-term: overdrafts, buying on credit, and debt factoring.

You should be able to identify the advantages and disadvantages of each of the above. For example, how quickly can the money be obtained? How much can be obtained? How much will need to be paid back? How much will the loan cost? How long will you have to pay it back in?

c)
- ◆ **Internal growth**: using sources of finance to increase production capacity.
- ◆ **Horizontal takeover**: taking over a business at the same stage of the production process.
- ◆ **Forward vertical takeover**: taking over one of the business's customers.
- ◆ **Backward vertical takeover**: taking over one of the business's suppliers.
- ◆ **Diversification**: moving into new products or new markets for the business's products.
- ◆ A **merger** is when businesses join together as equal partners to form a new business.
- ◆ A **takeover** is where one business buys another and it becomes part of the original business.

d)
- ◆ A change in management.
- ◆ The introduction of new technology.
- ◆ A change in the company's financial position.

Example

SAQ 5   a)   Briefly describe the main business objectives.

          b)   Identify the main stakeholders of an organisation, and describe how they can influence the organisation.

Answer to SAQ 5

a)   ◆   **Survival**: to make sure the business can continue to operate.

     ◆   **Growth**: to expand the business in its existing market or to move into new markets.

     ◆   **Profit maximisation**: to make as much profit as possible from existing resources.

     ◆   **Sales maximisation**: to sell as much as possible in order to increase the business's market influence.

     ◆   **Social/corporate responsibility**: to be aware of the needs of the community within which the company operates and to act accordingly.

     ◆   **Provide a service**: to provide a service for the public.

These are just a few of the main objectives. There are many more.

b)   ◆   Owners and investors: They can invest more money or take their money out of the business.

     ◆   Management and owners: They make the decisions that determine whether or not the business is a success.

     ◆   Employees: They can be more motivated or less motivated to work hard, and can take industrial action.

     ◆   Customers: They can decide to buy or not buy, and they can complain to consumer protection agencies/groups.

     ◆   Banks and suppliers: They can decide whether or not to do business with the organisation, and what credit terms, discounts and interest rates to offer.

     ◆   Government: It will vary tax rates, introduce new legislation, etc.

     ◆   Society/community: Members can complain to local and national government, pressure groups, etc.

Internal Assessment

You will be asked to describe how businesses in the private and the public sector are financed, owned and controlled.

You will then be asked to identify the stakeholders of an organisation, and say how they can have influence over the organisation.

Finally you will be asked to describe how the external factors of socio-cultural influences, technological influences, economic influences, political influences, and competitive affect the operation of an organisation.

Chapter 3

BUSINESS ENTERPRISE: BUSINESS INFORMATION AND ICT

What You Should Know

Sources of information	Primary, secondary, internal and external information.
Types of information	Qualitative and quantitative information.
Characteristics of good information	Accuracy, timeliness, completeness, appropriateness, availability, cost, objectivity and conciseness.
ICT in business	Characteristics and uses of current examples of ICT (information and communication technology) and telecommunications technology. Uses of ICT Costs and benefits of ICT
Business software	Characteristics and uses of business software. Data protection legislation. Costs and benefits of software.

Example

SAQ 1   Describe the main sources of information for an organisation.

Answer to SAQ 1

- **Primary information:** Information that has been collected and processed by the organisation.
- **Secondary information:** information that has been collected and processed by another person or organisation.
- **Internal information:** information that comes from within the business.
- **External information:** information that comes from outside the business.

Information that the business has collected itself is usually much more reliable, but it can be expensive to collect.

Example

SAQ 2   Briefly describe the two main types of information.

Answer to SAQ 2

◆ **Qualitative information:** information that is based on people's feelings and opinions.

◆ **Quantitative information:** information that is based on factual data that can be measured; it is usually expressed in numerical terms.

Example

SAQ 3   Outline the main characteristics of good information.

Answer to SAQ 3

◆ **Accurate**: containing no errors.

◆ **Timely**: up-to-date and available when needed.

◆ **Complete**: nothing missing.

◆ **Relevant**: about what the user needs to know.

◆ **Available**: accessible when needed.

◆ **Cost**-effective: does not cost too much to obtain.

◆ **Objective**: free from any bias.

◆ **Concise**: easily and quickly understood by the decision maker.

Example

SAQ 4   Identify the main types of ICT used in business.

Answer to SAQ 4

- Mainframe computers.
- Desktop computers.
- Laptops.
- Palm-held computers.
- Networks.
- E-mail.
- Multimedia.
- Internet.
- Wireless technology.
- Mobile phones.

You should be able to describe these and identify their costs and benefits. Remember that costs can include crashes and breakdowns, loss of information and hacker attacks.

Example

SAQ 5   Identify the main types of software used in business.

Answer to SAQ 5

- Word processors.
- Spreadsheets.
- Databases.
- Videoconferencing software.
- Fax software.
- Electronic point-of-sale software.
- Presentation and interactive slide shows.
- Desktop publishing.
- Management decision-making packages.

You should be able to describe these and their costs and benefits. Remember that the costs will include training costs, and lower productivity as users learn how to use the software properly.

Internal Assessment

You will be asked to identify primary, secondary, internal and external sources of information, and write about how reliable and valuable they are.

Then you will be asked to identify types of information technology and the costs and benefits of each.

Lastly, you will be asked to identify different types of business software and write about their costs and benefits.

The Internet

There have been an increasing number of questions in the examination regarding the use of the internet as a business tool, and there are some topics which you should make sure you know about.

E-commerce

Increasingly businesses are having to set up their web sites with the availability to shop on-line. This has been a major growth area of business particularly in Scotland, where working mothers and wives find it a very convenient way of shopping.

The web site should be easy to find and easy to use for the customer. They have to be 'live' (constantly updated) with full information on products including prices and pictures. Clever businesses will buy the domain names of all the possible mis-spellings of their names. (Try this yourself and see, but remember to use the internet responsibly.)

The web site should be secure as this is the thing that most puts people off shopping on-line.

Make sure you have a note of the costs and benefits of e-commerce for both the organisation and the customer.

Remember that the internet is also a very useful research tool. You can build up a database of your customers, and look at the competitors' web sites to find out what they are up to. Vast amounts of market information are available at low cost.

BUSINESS ENTERPRISE: DECISION-MAKING IN BUSINESS

What You Should Know ✔

The nature of decisions	Setting and achieving of objectives.
Types of decision	Strategic, tactical and operational decisions.
The role of managers	Interpersonal, informational and decisional roles. Managerial responsibilities: plan, organise, command, communicate, coordinate, control, delegate and motivate.
The decision-making model	Identification and setting of objectives, gathering of information, analysis of information, devising of solutions, selection from alternatives, communication of the decision, implementation of the decision, evaluation of the decision; influence of ICT on decision-making.
SWOT analysis	Identification of strengths, weaknesses, opportunities and threats. Drawing of conclusions and justification of conclusions.
Problems of the decision-making model	Time, ability to collect information, generation of solutions, creativity.

Example

SAQ 1   Discuss the three main types of decisions that managers may make.

Answer to SAQ 1

Strategic decisions

◆   These are long-term decisions about where the organisation wants to be in the future.

Example continued ➤

Example *continued*

- They are often made by the most senior managers and the owners of the organisation.
- They do not go into great detail about how the decisions will be implemented.
- Major policy statements represent strategic decisions.
- There are a large number of variables to consider when thinking about the future of the organisation, and the decisions are therefore not routine.

The **mission statement** summarises the strategic aims of the business.

Tactical decisions

- These are short-term decisions about how the strategic decisions are going to be implemented.
- They are often made by middle managers within the organisation, in finance, operations, human resources and marketing.
- They are based on achieving the goals or the aims of the organisation.
- They go into detail about what resources will be needed and how they will be used to achieve the aims.
- They are subject to change as political, economic, socio-cultural, competitive and technological factors change.

Operational decisions

- These are the day-to-day routine decisions.
- They can be made by all levels of management, but they are mostly made by lower-level managers and supervisors.
- They are made in response to relatively minor but sometimes important problems that arise each day or week, so they are routine and repetitive.

Example

SAQ 2   Briefly outline the constraints that are placed on decision-making.

Answer to SAQ 2

Internal constraints

◆   The finance available.

◆   Company policy.

◆   The employees' abilities and attitudes.

External constraints

◆   UK Government and EU legislation.

◆   Competitors' behaviour.

◆   Lack of new technology.

◆   The economic environment.

Example

SAQ 3   a)   Identify the three main roles that managers play within an organisation.

b)   Describe the main functions of management.

Answer to SAQ 3

a)   ◆   **Interpersonal role**: the relationships that a manager has to have with others.

◆   **Informational role**: the collecting and passing on of information.

◆   **Decisional role**: the making of various kinds of decision.

b)   ◆   **Plan**: Look ahead, see potential opportunities or problems, devise solutions, set targets, and set aims and strategies.

◆   **Organise**: Arrange for the resources of the organisation to be there when people need them, and acquire additional resources if necessary.

◆   **Command**: Issue instructions, motivate staff, and display leadership.

◆   **Co-ordinate**: Make sure that everyone is working towards the same goals, that all the work being done fits together, and that people are not duplicating work or working against each other.

◆   **Control**: Look at what is being done, check it against what was expected, and make any necessary adjustments. (This is the monitoring and evaluating role of management.)

◆   **Delegate**: Give subordinates the authority to carry out tasks. (This helps with motivation and reduces the manager's workload. The overall responsibility still lies with the manager who delegated the authority.)

◆   **Motivate**: Encourage staff through team working and participation in decision-making, and by giving them some powers.

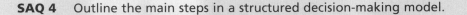

Example

SAQ 4   Outline the main steps in a structured decision-making model.

Answer to SAQ 4

◆ Identify the problem. (Set the aims.)

◆ Identify the objectives. (What is it that we want to achieve?)

◆ Gather information. (Good information leads to good decision making. Extensive use of internal and external information is required.)

◆ Analyse the information. (Study the information you have collected.)

◆ Devise various solutions. (Decide on a number of courses of action that you can take that will meet the aims.)

◆ Select from the solutions. (Select the solution that you think will be the one mostly likely to meet the aims of the organisation.)

◆ Communicate the decision. (If everybody knows what they are doing and why, they will be far more motivated to succeed.)

◆ Implement the decision. (Arrange for the necessary resources to be put into place.)

◆ Evaluate. (Using the information you have collected on how the process is going, compare this with what was expected to happen.)

Example

SAQ 5   a)   What are the main internal factors in a SWOT analysis?

b)   Describe the main external factors in a SWOT analysis.

c)   How will using a SWOT analysis benefit an organisation?

Answer to SAQ 5

a)   The internal factors (strengths and weaknesses) are the things that the organisation has control over. They relate to the resources of the organisation, or the factors of production.

Example continued ➤

Example *continued*

> ◆ Human resources: The workforce, including all levels of management, represent an investment by the organisation.
>
> ◆ Capital: A profitable business will have money available to carry out changes it needs to make to respond to changes in the market. Assets represent investment in the organisation by the owners. The higher the level of this investment, the more attractive the organisation is to potential investors and banks.
>
> ◆ Marketing: This includes the organisation's product range, its marketing mix, its distribution network, and its production processes.

b) The organisation cannot directly control its external influences (opportunities and threats). These influences come from the business environment in which the organisation operates. They can be grouped under these headings.

> ◆ Political. ◆ Technological.
>
> ◆ Economic. ◆ Competitive.
>
> ◆ Socio-cultural.

Looking at these areas is also known as PEST (political, economic, social and technological) analysis and STEP (social, technological, economic and political) analysis, which organisations often carry out in conjunction with SWOT analysis, as it allows for a better view of the business environment.

Note that some threats may also be opportunities, depending on how the organisation reacts to them.

c) The strengths will show areas where the business is currently doing well, and where possibilities for the future exist. The weaknesses will show areas to which attention needs to be paid now in order to make sure that the organisation survives. Opportunities have to be assessed carefully to make sure that the business makes the best of them.

SWOT analysis should not be thought of as a 'one-off' process. The conclusions drawn should be evaluated to make sure that the decisions were correct. Carrying out another SWOT analysis will let the business see if its conclusions were correct.

Example

SAQ 6 Describe the benefits and drawbacks of using a structured decision-making model.

Answer to SAQ 6

Drawbacks

◆ The time taken: If a solution is needed in a hurry, using the model can take too long.

◆ The ability to collect all the information needed: It is not always possible to get hold of all the good information needed to make the best decisions.

◆ The problems of generating solutions: It may be difficult to come up with a number of options.

◆ Lack of creativity: Managers may not be able to come up with imaginative alternatives.

Benefits

◆ The time taken: Because the process of going through each of the steps takes some considerable time, decisions are not rushed.

◆ The quality and quantity of information used: Care is taken in gathering, checking and analysing information. Using the best information available creates the best chance of the decision being the right one.

◆ Alternative solutions: The generation of various options allows for some creativity to be included in the decision. It also allows for fall-back plans to be made should the original decision turn out to be not working.

Example

SAQ 7 Identify two other aids to decision-making.

Answer to SAQ 7

◆ **Brainstorming**: A group meets to try to come up with as many solutions to a problem as possible.

◆ **Benchmarking**: The organisation compares what it does with what the very best organisations do.

Internal Assessment

You will be asked to identify the objectives of an organisation, and justify why you think these would be objectives. You will then be asked to identify strategic, tactical and operational decisions for the organisation.

Next you will be asked to write about the role of managers in decision-making, and in particular how they use the decision-making model, and how the success of the organisation is based on how effective its decision-making is.

The third part of the assessment deals with SWOT analysis, and you will be asked to prepare a SWOT analysis based on a case study. Remember that strengths and weaknesses are internal to the organisation, and it has control over them. Opportunities and threats are possibilities for the future, and are external to the organisation.

PART 2

Business Decision Areas

Chapter 5

BUSINESS DECISION AREAS: INTERNAL ORGANISATION

What You Should Know ✓

Grouping of activities	Grouping by function, product/service, customer, place/territory, technology and line/staff.
Functional activities	Marketing, human resources, finance, operations, and research and development.
Forms of organisational structure	Hierarchical, flat, formal, informal, matrix, entrepreneurial, centralised and decentralised structures.
Aspects of organisational structure	Organisation charts, spans of control, organisational culture, changes in structure, roles and responsibilities of management, downsizing, outsourcing, and empowerment.

Example

SAQ 1
  a) Discuss the advantages and disadvantages of functional groupings.

  b) Describe what is meant by product/service grouping and identify the advantages and disadvantages of using this grouping.

  c) Describe what is meant by customer grouping and discuss its advantages and disadvantages.

  d) Describe the advantages and disadvantages of using place/territory grouping.

  e) Briefly describe what is meant by technology grouping and its advantages and disadvantages.

  f) Describe what is meant by line/staff grouping.

Answer to SAQ 1

a) In **functional grouping**, the organisation is split into departments which represent the main functions of the business. (Businesses may have different kinds of functional department, depending on the type of business they are in.)

Example continued ➤

Example continued

Advantages

- The resources of the organisation of the business are better used.
- Staff become experts in their field.
- Career paths are created within the departments.
- Communication and cooperation within each department can be excellent.
- Team working improves.
- Decision-making is better.

Disadvantages

- Staff loyalty is to the department.
- There may be communication barriers between departments.
- There may be a slow response to changes in the business environment.
- Some decisions take a long time to make.
- Some problems cannot be solved by one department.

b) In **product/service** grouping, the organisation's activities are grouped around the various products and/or services that are provided by the organisation. Each product or service requires specialist knowledge and expertise, so it makes sense to gather all the staff with this knowledge and skill into one grouping.

Advantages

- Each division is a self-contained unit.
- Each member of staff in the division has a good level of knowledge about their specific product or service.
- It is easier to see which parts of the organisation are doing well and which are having problems.
- This grouping allows for a quicker response to external changes such as changes in customer wants.

Disadvantages

- Because each division requires its own support staff (in administration, finance, human resources management, etc.), there is bound to be duplication of resources, tasks and personnel within the organisation.

Example continued ➤

Example continued

◆ It is difficult for research and development and equipment to be shared across the organisation.

c) Some businesses put the customer first. Where the needs of different types of customer are important, the business will set itself up using **customer grouping**, in such a way that it has close contact with its customers.

Advantages

◆ Because the customers' needs are identified as a priority, customer loyalty can be built up.

◆ The customer gets the feeling of receiving a personal service even when dealing with large firms.

◆ The organisation can respond much more quickly to customers' needs.

Disadvantages

◆ The administration of such a grouping can be time-consuming, as individual customer needs take time and effort to meet.

◆ If there are staff changes, then the feeling of personal service can be lost.

◆ There is duplication of personnel and resources within the organisation.

d) Businesses whose customers are spread over a wide area of a country or over many countries often find it better to organise themselves around the place where their products are delivered, using **place/territory grouping**.

Advantages

◆ Local offices with local knowledge can cater for local clients' needs.

◆ Local offices can overcome problems caused by different countries having language and cultural differences.

◆ Because the local office is accountable for the area, it can be held accountable for success or failure in that area.

Example continued ➤

Example continued

- Customer loyalty can be built up using a local personal service.
- A local office is more responsive to changes in customer needs.

Disadvantages

- Administration can be time-consuming.
- If there are staff changes, then continuity of personal contact is lost.
- There is duplication of personnel and resources within the organisation.

e) In **technological grouping**, activities are grouped around the technological requirements for the product, mostly with respect to its manufacture or the process of delivery to the customer.

Advantages

- The degree of specialisation in the production process can be increased.
- Problems with the technology can be easily identified.

Disadvantages

- Staff have to be highly trained.
- These industries are very capital-intensive.

f) In **line/staff grouping**, the activities of the business can be separated into two types: core activities and support activities. **Core activities** are those that are the main purpose of the business. **Support activities** are those activities that are needed to make sure that the businesses operates properly.

The core activities are carried out by **line departments**. They are directly involved in the production of the goods or services that the organisation provides. The departments engaged in support activities, such as human resources management, finance, and research and development, are called **staff departments**. They provide specialist support and advice to the line departments, to help them with their operations.

Example

SAQ 2 a) List the main characteristics for each of the main types of organisational structure: hierarchical, flat, matrix, and entrepreneurial.

b) Compare centralised and decentralised organisational structures.

Answer SAQ 2

a) **Hierarchical structure**

- Each level of management represents a layer of authority.
- There is a great deal of control within this structure.

Example continued ➤

Example continued

- Each level of management has certain decision-making powers that they can pass down the structure to their subordinates.
- The information that is needed to make the decisions flows back up the chain of command through the hierarchical structure.
- Each person within the structure has a clearly defined role and tasks to perform.
- The tasks are often highly specialised.
- Communication can be slow, as the information makes a stop at each level on the way up the hierarchy and on the way down.
- The set roles and procedures within this structure do not allow it to adapt or change very quickly.
- This inability to change quickly makes the business vulnerable to changes in its market.

Flat structure

- There are few levels of management.
- This can be achieved through de-layering. (**De-layering** is the process of stripping out levels of management and thereby flattening the organisation.)
- The number of layers that information has to pass through is reduced, making it much quicker for information to flow up and down the organisation.
- Gathering information and consulting staff takes less time, and so some decisions can be made more quickly.

Matrix structure

- This structure tends to be used when the business is involved in a number of large projects (for example a construction firm that builds bridges, new schools, hospitals, etc., or a business that has a few large customers, such as a supplier to the oil industry).
- Teams are formed with staff from all, or most, of the functional departments.

Example continued ➤

Example *continued*

♦ Each member of the team has his or her own specialist skills.

♦ It allows for multiskilling, and employees get the opportunity to develop skills and expertise in other areas.

♦ Individuals are allowed more freedom to use their talents effectively.

♦ There may be a team leader, but usually a team has no hierarchy, and all the members have the same level of authority and responsibility.

Entrepreneurial structure

♦ Small businesses tend to have only one or two main decision-makers, who are usually the owners. Other staff may be consulted, but they often have little input into the decision-making process.

♦ Some larger businesses also adopt this structure (for example the editors of daily newspapers have to make decisions very quickly, and rely on their own expertise with respect to what should appear in each day's edition).

♦ The problem with this structure is that it relies too heavily on key decision-makers. The stresses involved often mean that they can only deal with their workload effectively for a relatively short period of time.

♦ As small businesses grow, they usually change their structure, employing more key staff so that the workload can be shared and the stresses reduced.

b) **Centralised structures**

♦ Centralised structures rely heavily on a number of key individuals who make most of the decisions within the organisation.

♦ Hierarchical structures are often highly centralised in terms of decision-making.

Decentralised structures

♦ Decentralized structures offer many of the benefits of flat structures while still retaining an effective level of overall management control.

♦ More of the decision-making is left to middle and lower management levels.

♦ The lower management levels have more power. However, the overall responsibility still lies with senior management.

There are distinct advantages to decentralisation.

♦ It allows the organisation to be more responsive to changes in the market or environment in which it operates. The people making the decisions are much closer to their customers, and have a better knowledge of their customers' needs and what is possible within their departments.

♦ Delegation to and empowerment of staff helps them to develop their professional skills and gives them more opportunities to display their own abilities.

♦ Having the power to make decisions means that staff who are aware of their customers and market can prepare for possible changes in advance.

Example

SAQ 3 a) Why are organisation charts useful?

b) Describe what is meant by 'span of control' and discuss the factors that affect it.

c) Why is organisational (corporate) culture important?

d) Identify the advantages and disadvantages of outsourcing.

Answer to SAQ 3

a) ◆ New members of staff can immediately see who they report to, and can identify the other members of their department.

◆ Each member of staff is included, and the chart shows which department he or she works in, their job title, who they report to, and what they are responsible for.

◆ Customers and suppliers can easily identify the various functional departments and identify who to contact in that department.

◆ Senior managers have an overview of the whole organisation, and can identify where problems with communications may occur, either up and down the hierarchy or between departments.

b) ◆ The **span of control** is the number of people who work directly for a manager or supervisor.

◆ The size of the span of control is important, because the bigger the span, the less supervision or control can take place.

The span of control is dependent on the following factors.

◆ The interpersonal and leadership skills of the manager.

◆ The skills and abilities of the staff.

c) ◆ Staff can be influenced by the actions and motivation of management. A positive leadership style should quickly lead to a positive attitude in the staff.

◆ The values of the organisation as a whole are dictated by the actions and communications of the management.

◆ The physical environment in which staff work affects how the staff act.

◆ Other environmental factors that can influence an organisation's culture are a dress code or the wearing of a staff uniform.

d) **Advantages**

◆ The organisation can concentrate on its core activities.

◆ The businesses outsourced to are specialists.

◆ They may have specialist equipment that can do the job better.

◆ The organisation does not need to employ staff to do the outsourced work.

Example continued ➤

Example *continued*

- The specialist firm may be able to produce at a lower cost.
- Outsourcing allows for downsizing of the organisation.
- The organisation may be more able to take on extra work or rush orders.

Disadvantages

- The organisation loses a certain amount of control over that part of its business.
- There may be communication problems.
- The specialist firm may gain access to confidential financial information.

Internal Assessment

You will be asked to describe and give an example of the various types of functional grouping.

Then you will be asked to identify the various types of structure that an organisation might have, and the advantages and disadvantages of each.

Chapter 6

BUSINESS DECISION AREAS: MARKETING

What You Should Know

The marketing concept	Marketing as a strategic activity: identifying, anticipating and satisfying consumer demands. Types of market, product and market orientation. Government influence: monopolies and mergers, fair trading, competition and consumer protection. Marketing environment: consumers, technology and economic forces.
The marketing mix	Price: long-term and short-term pricing strategies. Product: product portfolio/mix, product life cycle, extension strategies. Place: channels of distribution, roles of wholesalers, retailers and agents, types of retailers. Promotion: advertising, sales promotion, public relations, exhibitions and trade fairs, merchandising, direct mail and personal selling.
Target markets	Market segmentation. Methods of segmenting markets. Niche marketing. Market share and market growth.
Market research	Market research techniques: desk and field research, surveys, questionnaires and interviews, test marketing. Assessment of customer requirements.

Example

SAQ 1 a) Describe what is meant by 'identifying', 'anticipating', and 'satisfying'.

b) Briefly outline the objectives of marketing.

c) Identify the two types of market, and describe the classifications of products that are sold to them.

d) Briefly describe product orientation and market orientation.

Example continued ➤

Example *continued*

 e) Identify the main UK legislation influencing marketing decisions.

 f) Identify and describe the main influences on the marketing environment.

Answer to SAQ 1

a) ◆ Identifying: What does the consumer want from a good or a service in terms of price, features, quality, colours, delivery, packaging, image, after-sales service, etc.?

 ◆ Anticipating: Businesses have to try and anticipate what consumers will want in the future.

 ◆ Satisfying: The business must produce the right product at the right price at the right time: otherwise the sale will be lost.

b) ◆ To increase sales revenue and profitability.

 ◆ To increase or maintain market share.

 ◆ To maintain or improve the image of the business, its brand or its products.

 ◆ To target a new market or a new segment of the market.

 ◆ To develop new and improved products.

c) **Consumer markets** are made up of individuals who buy goods or services for their own personal or domestic use.

 ◆ Convenience goods, or non-durable goods, are products that consumers normally use only once and then have to replace on a regular basis, such as newspapers and magazines, foodstuffs, and toiletries.

 ◆ Shopping goods, or durable goods, are longer-lasting and only need to be replaced after a number of years. Cars, washing machines and televisions are examples of durable goods.

 ◆ Speciality goods are things like cosmetics, fashion items, and speciality cars.

Example *continued* ➤

Example *continued*

Industrial markets can buy similar goods to those bought in consumer markets. For example, consumers use banking services and so do businesses. However, businesses also buy plant and machinery, raw materials, consumable supplies, and business services.

d) ◆ **Product-orientated business**: This type of business concentrates on the production process and the product itself rather than on trying to establish what it is that customer wants.

◆ **Market-orientated business**: This kind of business continually identifies, reviews and analyses consumers' needs. Products are developed in response to these changing consumer needs.

e) ◆ Trades Description Act 1968: The goods or services that consumers buy must do what the advertising claims that they can do.

◆ Monopolies and Mergers Act 1965: Firms should not use or abuse their market power to cause consumers to suffer.

◆ Fair Trading Act 1973 and Competition Act 1998: These try to ensure that businesses do not attempt to prevent competition in the marketplace.

◆ Consumer protection laws: These Acts aim to ensure that the products consumers buy are safe.

◆ Code of advertising practice: Any business undertaking advertising must conform to the British Code of Advertising, Sales Promotion and Direct Marketing, which states that advertisements must be legal, honest, truthful and not cause offence.

f) The Government is one of the external factors that affect the marketing environment, which is made up of the following influences and factors.

◆ Competition: All markets are subject to some competition. In order to sell in competitive markets, the manufacturer's product must have something that makes the customer decide to buy that product rather than one of its competitors. This is the product's **unique selling point** (USP).

Example *continued* ➤

Example *continued*

◆ Technology: The continuing development of technology means that in order to keep up with the competition or gain some competitive advantage, organisations have to use the latest technology available.

◆ Economic forces: During times of economic growth, consumers are willing to spend more money and feel more confident about their job security. Organisations spend more on developing and marketing new products. During recessions, consumers spend less, and organisations tend to concentrate on reducing production costs and prices. Interest and exchange rates also affect demand.

◆ Consumer demographics: This the study of the structure of the population in terms of age, sex, household income, buying patterns, and lifestyles.

◆ Age: Research shows that there is an increase in the number of people aged 65 and over in the UK. Demand for services in this area is increasing, particularly in health, leisure activities, holidays, and financial services.

◆ Gender: Males and females have different buying patterns.

◆ Household income: The disposable income (the income left after tax) of families in the UK has greatly increased over the years. This has led to a big increase in the demand for clothes, holidays, DIY products, cars, leisure services, and furnishings.

◆ Location: Consumers living in different parts of the country have different needs and spending patterns.

◆ Social class: The usual social grade classifications are the following.

A (upper or upper middle class): Senior managerial/professional: company directors, surgeons, professors.

B (middle class): Intermediate managerial/professional: bank managers, head teachers, accountants, lawyers.

C1 (lower middle class): Supervisory: shop managers, bank clerks, sales representatives, nurses.

C2 (working class): Skilled: electricians, heating engineers, mechanics.

D (working class): Semi-skilled: machine operators, slaters, drivers, call centre workers.

E (lowest subsistence level): Unskilled and low-paid: cleaners, porters.

◆ Lifestyle, taste, and fashion: Consumers' lifestyles influence what products they buy.

◆ Personality: Consumers' personalities dictate what products they are interested in buying.

◆ Politics: Many consumers have strong political views, and this can influence their purchases.

Example

SAQ 2 a) Briefly describe the long-term and short-term pricing strategies used in marketing.

b) Why do some businesses adopt a product portfolio/mix rather than relying on a single product?

c) Describe the stages in the product life cycle.

d) Identify extension strategies for the product life cycle.

e) Discuss the advantages and disadvantages of branding and own-brand labels.

f) List the factors that affect the choice of channel of distribution.

g) Describe the roles of the groups involved in possible channels of distribution.

h) List the main forms of promotion.

i) Describe the four main types of advertising.

j) Describe and give examples of sales promotions.

k) Describe the role of the public relations officer within an organisation.

Answer to SAQ 2

a) **Long-term pricing strategies**

- Low price: A business may decide to charge a price that is lower than those of its competitors.

- Market price: Setting the price at the market rate means that the business's prices are in line with those of its competitors.

- High price: A business may set a high price when it is offering high-quality, premium goods and services where image is important.

Example continued ➤

Example *continued*

Short-term pricing strategies

◆ **Skimming**: This consists of setting a high price at first, usually for a new product where there is little competition. Consumers are willing to pay a high price for the novelty value of the product. However, as more competition enters the market, the price will be lowered.

◆ **Penetration pricing**: This is used in order to introduce a product to an established market, and it allows the business to achieve sales and gain market share very quickly. It involves setting a low price, sometimes at a loss, to attract customers. As the product becomes established, the business can increase the price.

◆ **Destroyer pricing**: This consists of setting an artificially low price to destroy the competition. The business will then probably be running at a loss in terms of these sales. However, as soon as the competition is eliminated, the price is reset at the market price or above.

◆ **Promotional pricing**: This is used to boost sales in the short term by lowering the price of the product. It can also be used to create interest in a new product.

◆ **Demand-orientated pricing**: The price varies with the demand for the product.

b) ◆ Each of the products in the portfolio will be at a different stage in its life cycle.

◆ This allows the business to spread its investment across a range of products, thereby reducing the level of risk.

◆ Profit levels can be relatively stable, making the business easier to manage.

c) **The development stage** is when the product starts its life.

◆ Get the idea.   ◆ Obtain any necessary patents.

◆ Analyse the idea.   ◆ Work out a price.

◆ Make a prototype.   ◆ Find finance for the launch.

◆ Test the prototype.   ◆ Advertise the product.

◆ Make any necessary changes.

At the introduction stage, the product is launched onto the market.

During the growth stage, consumers become more aware of the product and sales start to grow rapidly. It is during this stage that the product begins to become profitable.

At the maturity stage, the sales reach their peak.

◆ This is the highest level of sales that the product will achieve without the business taking some further action.

◆ Spending on advertising is much lower as the product is fully established in the marketplace.

◆ Any advertising is aimed at keeping up sales levels.

Example *continued* ➤

Example *continued*

- ◆ All the development costs should have been repaid, and the product is at its most profitable.
- ◆ The profits can then be used in part to fund development of new products.

In the decline stage, sales and profits start to fall, and the business's replacement products should be in the growth stage.

d) ◆ Promote more frequent use of the product.

- ◆ Develop new markets for existing products.
- ◆ Find new uses for existing products.
- ◆ Develop a wider range of products.
- ◆ Develop styling changes.

e) **Branding** can be a very successful marketing tool, and it is widely used by businesses to create USPs and emotional selling propositions (ESPs).

- ◆ The business chooses one or more words and/or symbols, and registers them so that they can only be used on its products.
- ◆ It then designs a marketing strategy to distinguish its products from all other similar products by using the brand.
- ◆ A business can create a form of product differentiation by using branding.

Benefits

- ◆ A well known brand generates instant recognition of the product by the customer.
- ◆ Brand loyalty can be established.
- ◆ Branding can lead to repeat purchases.
- ◆ It leads to a stable level of demand for the product.
- ◆ It allows for better production planning.
- ◆ It is very difficult to get consumers to switch brands.

Drawbacks

- ◆ It takes a great deal of time to establish a brand.
- ◆ Promotion costs are high, and even after the brand has been established, the business needs to keep promoting it to maintain brand visibility.

Example *continued* ➢

Example continued

- ◆ A single unfortunate event with bad publicity can affect the whole range of samebrand products.
- ◆ The business has to be able to protect its brand name worldwide.

Own brands

- ◆ Any product that sells in high volumes can be considered for own-brand labelling.
- ◆ Own brands provide more choice for the customer.
- ◆ The manufacturer has a guaranteed sales contract with the retailer.
- ◆ The business is protected from direct bad publicity as the retailer's name is on the label.
- ◆ The retailer has the goods made to its own specification and at its own price.
- ◆ The cheaper own-brand products attract more customers and more sales within the store.
- ◆ Own-brand products may be seen by consumers as being of lower quality than established brand names.

f) How the product gets to the consumer is decided by a number of factors.

- ◆ The product.
- ◆ The market.
- ◆ Legal requirements.
- ◆ Buying habits.
- ◆ The business.

g) The channel of distribution can involve wholesalers, retailers, agents, and importers/exporters. Which if any of these are used depends on the product.

Wholesalers

- ◆ Wholesalers are a good source of market research and marketing information, and can provide services for the retailer that will attract sales.
- ◆ Wholesalers buy in bulk and break their stock down into smaller quantities for the retailer.
- ◆ Some wholesalers will finish the product off with respect to packaging and pricing, thus reducing the producer's costs.
- ◆ The wholesaler has to play its part in the marketing strategy. If it does not promote the product in the way the business wants, it could destroy the business's marketing mix.

Retailers

- ◆ Retailers offer a variety of goods and services from a number of producers.
- ◆ They store the goods on their premises, prepare them for sale, and display them for sale.
- ◆ They provide information for consumers through advertising, displays, and trained staff.

Example continued ➢

Example *continued*

- They may also offer credit facilities, hire purchase, after sales service, guarantees, and delivery for large items.

Agents

- Agents attract customers by carrying out promotional activities, and then they sell the product to the consumer.
- Many smaller car manufacturers use agents to sell their cars in foreign countries.

Importers/exporters

- Importers/exporters play an important role in identifying new or potential markets for products around the world.
- Their role is similar to that of an agent, in that they have a good knowledge of local markets around the world, and can generate sales through their own promotional activities.
- In many cases, importers/exporters act as retailers as well.

Direct selling

- Direct selling is common when the manufacturer is a small local business.
- It is also widely used when products have to be made individually to a customer's specific requirements.
- Direct selling is common in industrial markets.

h)
- Advertising.
- Sales promotions.
- Exhibitions and trade fairs.
- Public relations.
- Merchandising.
- Direct mail.
- Personal selling.

i)
- **Informative advertising**: This is used to pass information to the consumer about new or improved products, or to give information about a technical product.
- **Persuasive advertising**: This is an attempt by manufacturers to get customers to buy their product.
- **Corporate advertising**: This promotes the whole company rather than individual products or services.
- **Generic advertising**: A number of advertisers or the whole industry gets together to promote the industry rather than individual products or services.

j) **Promotions into the pipeline** are designed to encourage wholesalers or retailers to take more stock, and they include the following.

Example *continued* ➤

Example continued

- Dealer loaders (for example when a retailer is given six boxes for the price of five).

- Point-of-sale displays, posters, and video cassettes.

- Dealer competitions that the dealers can enter to win prizes.

- Training for a shop's staff, to enable them to deal more effectively with customer enquiries.

- Sale or return terms (if the business does not sell all its stock, it can return it without charge).

- Extended credit, so that the shop does not have to pay for the products straight away.

Promotions out of the pipeline are promotions that give a direct benefit to the consumer to encourage them to make the purchase. They include the following.

- Free samples or trial packs that are given away in-store or with other products.

- Bonus packs.

- Price reductions.

- Premium offers where one product is given away free when the customer buys another.

- In-store demonstrations or tasting.

- Merchandising.

The benefits that are gained from sales promotions tend to be short-term, and they must be combined with other elements of the marketing mix if they are to be successful in the longer term.

k) ◆ Public relations is how the organisation communicates at a corporate level with the rest of the community.

- The community includes the public, the press, the Government, and shareholders.

- The communications are planned by the organisation in order to enhance its image.

Example continued ➤

Example continued

The role of the public relations department is an important one, and it may involve any of the following.

◆ Issuing press statements.

◆ Making charitable donations.

◆ Sponsoring events.

◆ Arranging for product endorsement by well known personalities.

Example

SAQ 3 a) Compare mass marketing and differentiated marketing.

b) Why do businesses segment their markets?

c) Describe what is meant by niche marketing.

Answer to SAQ 3

a) **Undifferentiated (mass) marketing**

◆ Undifferentiated marketing is where one product is sold to the entire market.

◆ There are very high-volume sales, so the manufacturer can benefit from economies of scale.

◆ There is usually a lot of competition in the marketplace.

Differentiated marketing

◆ Differentiated marketing is where businesses offer different products to various groups within the total market.

◆ This is done by modifying products to suit the different needs of various types of customer.

Example continued ➤

Example continued

b) ◆ Businesses are able to use differentiated marketing when they segment their markets.

◆ The whole market is split into various groups whose members have similar wants and needs.

◆ The business can produce goods and services specifically for those groups.

◆ The business can more closely meet the needs of customers, and so is more likely to make a sale.

◆ Businesses can dominate specialist parts of the market for their product.

c) ◆ Niche marketing is where a business aims a product at a particular, often very small, segment of the market.

◆ Customers needs and wants can be clearly identified.

◆ The niche market can be a local market or a small national market.

◆ Niche markets are often too small to accommodate two or more firms in competition.

◆ Large national firms that decide to enter a niche market can often force other businesses out of the market.

◆ Niche markets often suffer from larger and more frequent swings in consumer spending than larger markets.

Example

SAQ 4   a) Why do firms carry out market research?

b) Compare the advantages of using field research and desk research.

Answer to SAQ 4

a) The business may want to know any of the following.

◆ What types of consumer are buying the product.

◆ What the consumers think of the product.

◆ What prices consumers are prepared to pay for the product.

◆ What competition exists in the market and what potential competition there is.

◆ What types of packaging and promotion are most appropriate.

◆ How best to distribute the product and where to sell it.

◆ Whether any legal restrictions or regulations apply to the product.

Example continued ➤

Example continued

b) **Advantages of field research**

◆ The information is up-to-date.

◆ It is collected for the exact purpose required.

◆ It is not available to competitors.

◆ It gives the organisation a competitive advantage over its rivals.

Primary information is usually gathered through a survey.

Advantages of desk research

◆ It is cheaper and easier to obtain than primary data.

Disadvantages of desk research

◆ The information is historical.

◆ It has been collected for another purpose.

◆ It may also be available to competitors.

Internal Assessment

You will be asked to describe the role and importance of marketing for an organisation, and then to describe product and market orientation.

Next you will be asked to identify examples of the elements of the marketing mix, and then to write about target markets, undifferentiated markets, differentiated markets, niche markets, and market segmentation.

You will be asked to write about the product portfolio of an organisation and its importance when bringing out new products, and then about strategies that can be used for extending the product life cycle.

Finally, you will be asked to write about the importance of carrying out market research, and then to explain the various types of market research that can be used.

BUSINESS DECISION AREAS: FINANCIAL MANAGEMENT

What You Should Know

Cash flow	Use of cash flow statements, and their purpose and interpretation.
Financial reporting	Components of final accounts: trading and profit and loss accounts, and balance sheets.
Ratio analysis	Profitability, liquidity and efficiency ratios.
Budgets	Uses of budgets.

Example

SAQ 1 Describe the role of finance within the business.

Answer to SAQ 1

◆ Payment of wages and salaries.

◆ Payment of accounts/invoices.

◆ Maintenance of financial and cost records.

◆ Production of financial statements/accounts.

◆ Provision of cost information for decision-making.

Example

SAQ 2 Explain why businesses use cash flow statements.

Answer to SAQ 2

◆ The statements are used to identify where money is coming from and where it goes.

◆ They have to be prepared as part of the year end accounts.

◆ Good cash management is essential for business success.

◆ The statements are used to highlight areas of waste or theft.

Example

SAQ 3 Identify the main parts of the final accounts of a business.

Answer to SAQ 3

- ◆ Trading account.
- ◆ Profit and loss account.
- ◆ Balance sheet.
- ◆ Cash flow statement.

Example

SAQ 4 Identify profitability, liquidity and efficiency ratios, and then describe what factors change them.

Answer to SAQ 4

Ratio	Formula	Changed by these factors
Gross profit ratio	gross profit/sales × 100%	Selling price Cost of goods sold
Net profit ratio	net profit/sales × 100%	Selling price Cost of goods sold Expenses
Ratio of gross profit to cost of goods sold	gross profit/cost of goods sold × 100%	selling price cost of goods sold
Current ratio	current assets/current liabilities	The ability of the business to meet its short term debts
Acid-test ratio	current assets/current liabilities – stock	A more accurate short-term measure, as stock can be difficult to sell quickly at its current value
Return on capital employed	net profit/capital employed × 100%	The higher this is the better, as it shows how much profit is made for every £1 invested

Example

SAQ 5   What can profitability, liquidity and efficiency ratios be used for?

Answer to SAQ 5

◆   To compare performance with that in previous years.

◆   To aid the planning of the business.

◆   To compare performance with that of similar businesses.

Example

SAQ 6   Describe how a business uses budgets.

Answer to SAQ 6

◆   Business plans are usually expressed in financial terms.

◆   The master budget contains budgets for each of the departments.

◆   Sales, production and cash budgets are the most common types of budget.

Budgets can be used to do the following.

◆   Monitor and control the business.

◆   Set targets.

◆   Delegate authority without losing control.

Internal Assessment

You will have to identify cash flow problems from a cash flow statement, and then write about what problems this may cause for the organisation and what it should do to avoid them.

Next you will be asked to look at ratios for an organisation over two years or for two different businesses. You will be asked to write about the profitability, liquidity and efficiency ratios, comparing them for the two years or for the two organisations.

Lastly you will be asked to write about how budgets help management to plan for a business, and how they can be used to monitor and control the business.

The most common examination questions are based around the monitoring and control of the business through cash flow projections and budgets.

Cash flow

One of the main functions of the finance department is to ensure adequate cash is available to meet the organisation's objectives.

What You Should Know

You should know why cash flow problems arise such as too much money invested in stock or fixed assets or over trading.

You should also know how the business could resolve cash flow problems such as selling unused fixed assets, sale and leaseback, selling invoices to debt factors, etc.

Budgets

Budgets set targets for the managers within the business.

Students often focus on cash budgets, however, it is important to remember that budgets are used to control the **whole** business. All departments are given a budget which they should try to stick to.

All these budgets are part of a master budget which controls the whole business and is based on the expected sales and/or production. The point is, that if departments are not sticking to their budgets then it is very easy to see where problems are arising and take some action to make changes.

BUSINESS DECISION AREAS: HUMAN RESOURCES MANAGEMENT

What You Should Know

Changing patterns of employment	Gender balance, part-time and contract workers, and the role of the core workforce (key personnel).
Recruitment and selection	Job analysis, job descriptions, person specification, and internal and external recruitment. Selection methods: applications, CVs, interviews and testing.
Training and staff development	Benefits of training and staff development. Staff appraisal.
Employment relations	Main employee relations institutions: the Confederation of British Industry (CBI), the Trades Union Congress (TUC), the Advisory, Conciliation and Arbitration Service (ACAS), etc. Processes in employee relations and the management of employee relations: works councils, single-union agreements, grievance procedures and discipline procedures.
Employment legislation	Discrimination law, employment law, and health and safety legislation.

Example

SAQ 1 a) Describe the objectives of human resources management.

b) Identify and describe the various needs of workers within an organisation.

Answer to SAQ 1

a) ◆ To promote a policy of continuous staff development.

◆ To recruit, develop and retain people for current and future jobs.

◆ To manage employee relations, and maintain the commitment of the workforce.

◆ To design, implement and manage remuneration, rewards and appraisal schemes.

Example continued ➤

Example continued

- To maintain and improve the physical and mental well-being of the workforce by providing appropriate working conditions and health and safety conditions.

- To take account of all government legislation relevant to human resources management.

b)
- **Physiological needs** are for things such as food, clothing, shelter and warmth, and are satisfied by wages high enough to meet the weekly bills.

- **Safety needs** can be satisfied through job security, a contract of employment, membership of a trade union, and employment laws.

- **Emotional needs** are satisfied through team working, job rotation and social clubs.

- **Esteem needs** are satisfied by recognition for a job well done, promotion, merit awards, or a better job title.

- **Self-actualisation needs** are satisfied by promotion, more responsibility, ownership of company shares, or self-employment.

Example

SAQ 2 a) How have patterns of employment in the UK changed in recent years?

b) Describe the possible drawbacks of having a flexible workforce.

Answer to SAQ 2

a)
- Employees are only concerned with the core activities of the organisation. The core activities are those that directly achieve the organisation's objectives.

- Part-time jobs are much more common, owing to the workers' flexibility, higher levels of productivity, and lower cost.

Example continued ➤

Example continued

- Casual staff can be hired and released as and when they are needed.
- Contractual staff are staff who are employed on a fixed-term contract of one or two years, or agency staff. At the end of the contract, the employee is either released or offered a new contract.
- The number of women who are working increases continuously.
- With flexitime, workers only have to be at their workplace at certain core times of the day.
- 'Hot desks' are areas of the workplace that are set aside for staff who do not need office space all the time, for example salespeople.
- With modern communications equipment, many jobs can now be carried out at the worker's home and by teleworking.

b)
- The human resources department spends much more time recruiting staff and ensuring that enough staff are available.
- The amount of training required increases.
- When dealing with customers, continuity of staff is important.
- Non-core staff are less likely to be motivated towards achieving the organisation's goals and objectives.

Example

SAQ 3 a) Discuss the main steps in the recruitment process.

b) What methods are available for effective selection.

Answer to SAQ 3

a) **Job analysis**
- Does the vacancy actually exits?
- What are the main physical and mental elements of the job?
- What specific skills are required?
- Who would the job holder be responsible for, and who would they be responsible to?
- Where would the job holder work, and what would the main health and safety considerations be?

Job description/specification
- The job title.
- The overall purpose of the job.

Example continued ➤

Example *continued*

- The main tasks and responsibilities.
- The job holder's decision-making powers.
- Who the job holder is responsible for and to, and who they work with.
- The skills, qualifications and experience required to do the job.
- Where the job is based.
- The resources required to do the job.

The job specification can also include details of the pay and conditions available to the post holder.

Person specification

- The physical attributes that the successful candidate should have with respect to personal appearance etc.
- The skills, educational qualifications, training and experience that the candidate should have.
- The level of intelligence that is needed.
- The kind of personality that is preferred.
- The special skills that are required.

Internal recruitment (promoting from within)

- Internal recruitment can be cheaper.
- The person is already known to the organisation.
- The person will have benefited from the organisation's investment in training.
- Promotion can be a strong motivator for employees.

Some disadvantages of internal recruitment are the following.

- It restricts the number of applicants for the post.
- New workers can bring new skills and ideas to the organisation.

Example *continued* ➤

Example *continued*

◆ Any promotion will probably create another vacancy, which will then have to be filled.

External recruitment

◆ This can be done using any of the following.

◆ A Job Centre.

◆ An advertisement in a local or national newspaper.

◆ An employment agency.

◆ Trade journals.

◆ A head-hunting agency.

◆ The Internet.

b) ◆ Application forms give all the applicants the same questions and opportunities to describe themselves. This makes it much easier to compare information from a large number of candidates. The application forms are compared to the person specification to see which of them appear to match.

◆ Interviews are the most common way of making a final decision on who the successful candidate should be, based on their match with the person specification.

◆ Aptitude tests measure how good the applicant is at particular skills, for example mathematical skills, typing and shorthand, and driving.

◆ Psychometric tests measure the personality, attitudes and character of the applicant.

◆ Personality tests give an indication as to whether the applicant is a team player, and what team roles they would perform best.

Example

SAQ 4 a) Describe the main methods of staff training and development.

b) Identify the costs involved in training and development.

c) What are the benefits to an organisation of using a staff appraisal scheme?

Answer to SAQ 4

a) **Induction training**

◆ Induction training is given to all new employees.

◆ It explains what tasks they are expected to perform.

Example *continued* ➤

Example continued

- It helps them to develop an awareness of the organisation's policy and practices.
- It allows them to become familiar with their surroundings.

On-the-job training

- On-the-job training is given while the employee is doing the job.
- It consists of a more experienced employee showing the worker how to do a job.
- The more experienced employee may watch and offer advice and instruction while the other worker completes the task (coaching).
- The trainee may work in several departments or areas of the organisation, learning what each one does.

Off-the-job training

- The organisation may have its own training department.
- The employee may be sent on organised training courses.
- The employee may be able to obtain qualifications from a college or university.

Staff development

- Staff development allows all the workers to achieve the level of performance of the most experienced workers.
- It makes a wide pool of skills available to the organisation, now and in the future.
- It allows a knowledgeable and committed workforce that is highly motivated to be developed.
- It ensures that the organisation can deliver high-quality goods or services.

b)
- Costs of travel and subsistence.
- Cost of workers being away from their jobs.
- Cost of bringing in other staff to cover.

Example continued >

Example *continued*

c) ◆ Identifying future training needs.

◆ Considering development needs for the individual's career.

◆ Improving the performance of the employee.

◆ Providing feedback to the employee about his or her performance.

◆ Identifying individuals who have the potential for future promotion within the organisation, or who have additional skills that could be useful now or in the future.

Example

SAQ 5 a) Explain why good employee relations are important.

b) What should be included in employee relations policies?

c) Describe the main UK employee relations institutions.

d) Outline the main processes for employee relations.

e) Identify and describe the main instruments for managing employee relations.

Answer to SAQ 5

a) ◆ Good employee relations help to ensure that the organisation meets its objectives.

◆ Workers are usually much happier and more motivated and committed to the goals of the business when employee relations are good.

◆ The workers are more accepting of change.

◆ They are more flexible in their response to requests.

◆ They recognise the need for the organisation to achieve its objectives.

◆ Poor employee relations lead to a less cooperative workforce, more industrial action, and a poor image of the organisation among its customers.

b) ◆ The terms and conditions of employment for staff.

◆ Procedures for dealing with staff complaints (grievances), the disciplining of staff, and redundancy, including any agreed payments.

◆ The level of involvement of staff in decision-making.

◆ Trade union recognition (some businesses do not recognise trade unions).

◆ Collective bargaining procedures (discussions with trade unions on pay and conditions or changes to working practices for all employees).

Example *continued* ➤

Example *continued*

c) **Advisory, Conciliation and Arbitration Service (ACAS)**

- Provides impartial information and help to anyone with a work problem.
- Prevents and resolves problems between employers and their workforces, and helps to settle disputes.
- Settles complaints about employees' rights.
- Encourages people to work together effectively.

Employers' associations

- Employers' associations look after the interests of all the businesses in a particular industry.
- They can pressure the Government and may influence it.
- They can gather market research for the benefit of the whole industry.

The **Confederation of British Industry (CBI)** tries to represent the employers from all the UK industries.

The **Trades Union Congress (TUC)** represents all the UK trade unions.

Trade unions were set up to protect employees from unscrupulous employers and to provide a political voice for the working people of the UK.

d)
- **Negotiation**: The purpose of negotiation is to come to an agreement.
- **Consultation**: Consultation consists of discussions between employers and employees. No agreement is necessary, and the employer is under no obligation to take account of the views of the employees.
- **Arbitration**: The arbitrator is unbiased and neutral. They listen to both sides, gather other evidence as appropriate, and offer a solution.
- **Collective bargaining**: A trade union or other body negotiates with the employer on behalf of the employees, usually on pay or changes that are proposed in the workplace.

e)
- **Works councils:** A group of representatives from the workforce have the legal right to access information from management, and have joint decision-making powers on most matters relating to employees.
- **Single-union agreements**: One union represents all the workers in the workplace.
- **Grievance procedures**: A grievance procedure is followed when an employee has a complaint.
- **Disciplinary procedures**: Disciplinary procedures are taken against an employee by the employer when the employee is thought to have done something wrong.

Example

SAQ 6 What are the main legislative requirements of a UK business will respect to human resources?

Answer to SAQ 6

◆ Equal Pay Act 1970 was introduced to make sure that men and women would receive the same pay and conditions for doing 'broadly similar' work.

◆ The Sex Discrimination Act 1975 was introduced to ensure that men and women were treated equally and fairly at work.

◆ The Race Relations Act 1976 deals with discrimination against employees because of colour, race, nationality or ethnic origin.

◆ The Disability Discrimination Act 1995 deals with discrimination against an employee or potential employee because of their disability.

◆ A wide range of legislation covers employment law. In most cases it protects the workers from what are seen to be undesirable practices by employers. The main pieces of legislation are the Employment Act 1989, the Employment Relations Act 1999, the Employment Rights Act 1996, the Working Time Regulations 1998, and the National Minimum Wage Act 1998.

◆ Industrial tribunals are used when all other avenues have failed to settle a dispute between employers and their employees, and for cases of unfair dismissal.

◆ The Health and Safety at Work Act 1974 raises the standard of health and safety for all individuals at work, and protects the public whose safety may be put at risk by the activities of people at work.

Internal Assessment

The first part of the assessment deals with the recruitment procedures of job analysis, job description and person specification, and then asks you to write about internal and external sources of recruitment.

The second part covers selection, and deals with application forms, interviews, testing and references. It then asks you to write about the importance of good recruitment and selection processes, and how they help with the efficiency of the organisation.

The last part deals with the importance of employee relations and ways of ensuring good employee relations, and then asks about employee representation through trade unions, works councils, etc.

BUSINESS DECISION AREAS: OPERATIONS MANAGEMENT

What You Should Know

The operations process	Input, process, output.
	Production systems used in manufacturing: just in time (JIT) manufacturing etc.
	Stock control.
	Purchasing mix.
	Payment systems.
Distribution and delivery	Warehousing and storage, and transportation
Methods of production	Job, batch and flow production.
Factors that affect quality	Quality control, quality assurance, benchmarking, quality circles, and total quality management (TQM).

Example

SAQ 1   Describe the advantages and disadvantages of a just-in-time system.

Answer to SAQ 1

Advantages

- The costs of holding stock are reduced to minimum.
- Waste is removed from the system for materials that are becoming out-of-date or obsolete.
- More space is created for production.
- Money that was tied up in stock can be used elsewhere in the business.
- The business can develop closer relationships with its suppliers.

Disadvantages

- Production can be disrupted because supplies have not arrived in time, and this can lead to lost sales.
- The business has to depend on its suppliers and does not have as much time to check the quality of stock when it arrives, because it is needed straight away.
- A business cannot get discounts for buying in bulk, and transport costs increase, with many small loads arriving at the factory instead of a few big ones.
- There is more administration because orders are placed more often.
- Transport difficulties have a bigger impact on the business.

Example

SAQ 2 a) Describe the benefits to an organisation of using quality standards in production.

b) Describe the main quality assurance instruments used in production.

Answer to SAQ 2

a) ◆ The customers are given the product that they want, which leads to repeat sales and the possibility of brand loyalty.

◆ There are fewer complaints and returns of goods.

◆ The customer is assured of a quality product.

◆ The business can establish a benchmark for its product that will help it to improve the product.

b) **Quality assurance**

◆ Quality assurance is based on the prevention of errors, with checking taking place at each stage of the operation. The aim is to have zero defects.

◆ Standards are set and agreed. Staff work to these throughout the organisation.

◆ Systems for monitoring and controlling the system are put in place.

◆ After sales services are provided for customers.

◆ There has to be a high level of commitment and skill in the workforce.

TQM

◆ The customer is at the centre of operations. The aim is to meet customer requirements in terms of the product and quality.

◆ Quality chains are established, with everyone working to a set standard, the next person in the chain being the customer.

◆ TQM involves all of the workforce, and management must be committed to providing the resources necessary for it to succeed.

◆ The whole process must be monitored and controlled, and there must be a constant search for improvements (which is known as *kaizen* in Japan).

◆ Everyone in the process is responsible for their own performance.

Example

SAQ 3 a) Describe the main types of production and when they should be used.

b) Outline the factors that decide the type of production used.

Answer to SAQ 3

a) ◆ **Job production**: This is used for 'one-off' products made to the customer's specific requirements. It is usually used by small businesses and specialist manufacturers. Examples are wedding cakes, construction and tailor-made clothing.

◆ **Batch production**: A batch of similar products are made at the same time. They are all completed before another batch is made. The batches may vary in terms of materials, but the same basic production process is used. Batch production is commonly used in the food industry. For example Baxters produces batches of the different types of soup.

◆ **Flow production**: There is continuous production on a production line through various stages. Flow production is used in mass production when the same or very similar products are made. One example is electricity, which is continuously produced and supplied to customers. In car manufacturing, the same basic product can be changed slightly, for example there are various sizes of engine, various colours, etc.

b) ◆ The nature of the final product.

◆ The market size.

◆ The resources available to the business.

◆ The stage of development of the business.

◆ The availability of technology.

PART 3

Assessment

INTERNAL ASSESSMENT

For now, there are three methods of internal assessment:

- eight individual assessments for each of the units,
- or what are called 'holistic', assessments that cover a number of different units in the one assessment
- or a mixture of the two.

No matter which method your teacher or lecturer uses, what you need to know for each is the same as the 'performance criterion' (PC's – what has to be in the assessment) is the same for any method.

What we will do is look at the PC's for each unit in turn, then look at the questions you will be asked, and then look at what you should write as answers.

Unit 1: Learning Outcome One – Business in contemporary society

PC (a) – Comparison of the types of business organisation in the UK and their organisational objectives is accurate.

What you will be asked

For this assessment you will be asked to compare the types of business organisation in the UK. You will need to know how each type of business in owned and controlled, plus how each is financed. You may well be asked to pick an example from publicly funded and one from privately funded. There is also the possibility that you will be asked to pick one from the voluntary sector as well. You will be expected to give examples of each.

Common Mistakes

Many students confuse public limited companies with public sector organisations.

Remember

Remember – A public limited company is a private sector organisation. It is owned by shareholders who are private individuals and their main objective is to make profits, where as a public sector organisation is a government funded business whose main aim is to provide a service. Make sure you know the difference between them.

Marks will be given for each comparison of ownership, control and finance. To get full marks you must clearly show that you understand the differences between the different types of organisation, and you have to compare them in your answer.

Answer

The NHS is a public sector organisation, set up by the government and controlled by a local NHS trust, whereas BP are a public limited company owned by the shareholders and controlled by the Managing Director or Chief Executive and the Board of Directors. A sole trader on the other hand is a single person business owned and controlled by that person.

Each is financed differently. The NHS is financed by the government through taxation, while BP can gain finance through selling shares, debentures or bank loans. A sole trader will provide all the finance for their business either from their own pocket or by borrowing money from the bank.

PC (b) – Comparison of the relative influence of key stakeholders on different types of organisation is accurate.

What you will be asked
Here you will be asked to identify different stakeholders for different organisations, and then describe how they can influence the organisation.

The number you will be asked to identify will depend on the assessment you are given, however, you should be able to identify at least three stakeholders for each organisation.

Answer

Employees of a plc can take different forms of industrial action to influence the decisions they make, such as how much they will pay the employees. On the other hand, a local authority will have to take account of the people in the local community when deciding whether or not to close a local school as they can protest and if they don't get their way they can avoid voting for them in the next election.

Managers are also stakeholders, and their influence is through the quality of the decisions that they make which will determine how successful the business is.

PC (c) – Interpretation of factors affecting the operation of business enterprise is accurate in terms of their impact on an organisation.

Here you will have to explain how each of the external factors of socio-cultural, technological, economic, political, and competitive environment, can affect the operation of a business. You should be able to give one example for each.

Answer

Political – The introduction of new laws will affect the business. For example, an increase in the minimum wage will mean that some businesses will have to pay their employees more which could affect their profitability.

Economic – An increase in interest rates will make the cost of borrowing more expensive so businesses can afford to borrow less which means they may not be able to expand as they wanted to.

Socio-cultural – The fact that women now have far more economic power than ever before means that marketing and production have to be aimed to meet women's needs as much as men's.

Technological – The reduction in cost and availability of broadband means more people can shop from home. All businesses will have to arrange on-line shopping facilities if they wish to attract as many customers as possible.

Competitive – If a competitor introduces a new or better product the business will have to either bring out a similar product or reduce their prices to keep customers buying their product.

Learning outcome two – Business information and information and IT in business.

Assess the value of information and the application of information technology to business enterprise.

There are 3 PC's for this unit. What you will need to know will be much the same for all the assessments, however, what will be required may vary slightly from one assessment to another.

PC (a) – Assessment of different sources of information is accurate in terms of their reliability and value for particular business enterprises.

What you will be asked

In the first part of this assessment you will be asked to identify information from **primary**, **secondary**, **internal** and **external** sources, and justify or explain why this is an example for each of the sources. You should use different examples for each of the sources of information.

Answer

An example for primary information could be a customer survey. This is first hand information collected by the organisation and used for a particular purpose. This information is accurate and up-to-date.

An example of secondary information is a newspaper article. This information is collected by someone else for their own purpose and you are reusing it for your own different purpose.

An example of internal information is sales records. This information is produced within the business and is not available to anyone outside the organisation.

An example of an external source would be government statistics. This is information that is produced by the government which the business can use for its own purpose.

What you will be asked
The second part of this PC will ask you to assess the reliability and value of information derived from the sources you gave in the first answer. Use the examples above to provide an answer to this question.

Answer

The customer survey is obtained direct from the source, so you know how accurate it is, and you can go back to the original source and ask other questions. It will be appropriate to the needs of the organisation as they gathered it themselves for a particular purpose.

Newspaper article – This information may not be accurate or reliable and may contain bias.

Sales records – You know how accurate it is. However, it will be out of date but may give an indication of the level of future sales.

Government statistics – It is generally low cost but will be dated.

PC (b) – Assessment of main types of information technology is accurate with respect to their uses in business and their costs and benefits to business enterprise.

What you will be asked

Here you will be asked to identify a number of different types of technology and then describe the benefits of using this technology and the costs (not just money costs). You must show you understand why what you have said is a benefit will actually benefit the organisation.

There are no marks available for simply identifying the type of IT so you need to know the costs and benefits.

Answer

E-mail provides almost instant written communication with anywhere in the world protected by a password, this will reduce costs for telephone etc, and remove the delays caused by using letter mail services. A cost may be the loss of personal contact, either through meeting face to face or talking on the phone, which reduces the chance of good working relationships and increases the possibility of misunderstanding.

Laptops allow employees to work on the move or from home. Technology allows information to be transferred to and from the organisation instantly. The costs involved include the purchase costs of the laptop and its software.

Mobile phones allow employees to keep in touch with customers and their own organisation while on the move or while at home. They can be used to receive and send e-mails. The costs will include the network charges and the cost of calls and text messages.

PC (c) – Assessment of the uses of business software is accurate in terms of its potential applications to business activity and its costs and benefits to business enterprises.

What you will be asked

Here again you must identify a number of pieces of software and describe the costs and benefits of using them. Again there are no marks available for the identification of the software, but you still need to know them. It is better if you can identify the type of software rather than a brand name, for example a database package rather than 'Access'.

Answer

An electronic database allows you to store records electronically. Benefits include space saved, the ability to sort records into any order, and to filter them to show specific groups of records. This would allow managers to make better decisions by obtaining accurate, up-to-date information quickly and easily.

An example of a cost could be the cost of the system crashing and the information being lost or even becoming unavailable for a period of time. Loss of data would be very serious as it would mean essential information for decision-making is lost.

You could give similar answers for word processing and spreadsheet packages. For word processing benefits could include using text enhancement and mail merge, for spreadsheet benefits could include carrying out electronic calculations and running 'what if' analysis. For both, costs could include staff training to use the packages and the cost of updating software.

Learning outcome three – Decision making in business

There are four PC's (Performance Criteria) that must be covered in this topic. You will be expected to analyse the process of decision making in a business enterprise. To do this you will be given a detailed case study which you will have to read carefully. It is always a good idea to read them once, then read the questions, and then go through the case study again with a highlighter to note the pieces of text which you will need to answer the questions.

PC (a) – Analysis of different types of decision is accurate and related to the objectives of the organisation.

What you will be asked
There are two parts for PC (a), the first is to identify the objectives of the organisation.

Answer

This will be a private sector business so maximising profits will be an obvious choice. It is not an organisation in the Public Sector so providing a public service would not be a good choice.

Other answers you could give may include increasing market share, growth, social responsibility, profit etc.

However, you should remember that you will have to relate them to the business in the case study.

You should also justify your choice of objectives (explain why would it be an objective).

Answer continued ➤

Answer continued

Maximising profits would be an objective for this business because it would allow the firm to either use the profits to improve the business or to provide shareholders with larger dividends.

The second part will be to identify and analyse at least one each of strategic, tactical, and operational decisions. This will depend very much on what is in the case study, but the marks will be for the analysis as well as for identification.

It is difficult sometimes to differentiate between the different types of decisions, so your marks will be gained in explaining why you think it is that type of decision.

A tactical decision of the business is to open a new store. This is a tactical decision because it is a medium term decision designed to meet the business's objective of increasing market share. The more stores it has the more customers it will get.

PC (b) Analysis includes an accurate explanation of the role of managers in decision making in an organisation.

What you will be asked

You will be asked to describe the role of management in decision making for the business.

Answer

Much of your answer here should relate to the structured decision making model. How you answer the question again depends very much on the case study and the actual question you are asked.

You should start your answer:

Managers play an important role in decision making, because it is through their decisions that the business is actually able to meet its aims.

You may be asked to identify one of the managers in the case study and describe the role he or she played in the decision making process for the organisation. You could identify some of the steps in the structured decision making model from the text or you may simply have to list the steps, explaining each briefly.

PC (c) – Analysis includes the development and evaluation of a suitable SWOT analysis for a business enterprise.

What you will be asked
You will be asked to carry out a SWOT analysis of the organisation in the case study.

Answer

The answers here will depend on the case study. The important points to remember are that strengths and weaknesses are internal and are about the business itself, whereas opportunities and threats are external and relate to the business environment.

To make sure you get full marks you could relate the opportunities and threats to Political, Economic, Socio-cultural, Technological, and Competitive factors.

PC (d) – Analysis includes reasoned justification for conclusion drawn from the SWOT analysis.

Analyse, justify, and conclusions, are all words which cause problems for students in the internal and external exam.

You may have identified that there was a problem with the suppliers for the business in your SWOT. This would be part of your analysis of the case study. It would be a conclusion that something should be done to rectify this. Justification for your conclusion would be that problems with suppliers could affect production and therefore sales.

UNIT TWO – BUSINESS DECISION AREAS Learning outcome one – Internal Organisation

PC (a) – Analysis of organisational structure is accurate with respect to the grouping of activities within an organisation

What you will be asked
You will be asked about the organisational groupings – Functional, Product/Service, Customer, Place/Territory (Geographical), and Technological.

It is unlikely that there would be any marks available for naming them in the assessment, but it is possible that marks will be available in the final exam so you should always be able to identify them.

The marks available vary between assessments, however, each question will allow you to show

that you can explain what each grouping is and can identify an appropriate example, asking you about the advantages and disadvantages of some or all of the groupings.

Using an example is probably the best way to show that you know **and** understand what you are writing about. Good examples will always give you a better chance of achieving full marks, and you may even be given some examples in the text.

Answer

When answering about functional groupings, identify an organisation that has, or is likely to have, all or most of the functional departments.

This will show that you know what the functional areas are, and that your example is organised into departments around these functions (marketing, human resources, finance, and operations).

The next part is to show that you know why they decided to organise this way.

So for the example of functional groupings you would have to describe the advantages of organising this way. You should also be able to list the disadvantages of each grouping.

PC (b) – Internal organization of a business enterprise is analysed accurately and related to different forms of organizational structure.

What you will be asked
The question will be about the different types of structure an organisation may have.

Answer

You should be able to identify at least four: Tall (pyramid), Flat, Entrepreneurial, and Matrix. Again much depends on the question that you are asked, however, you should be able to describe the advantages and disadvantages of each type of structure, and explain when each would be an appropriate structure for an organisation.

For example, an entrepreneurial structure would be most suitable for a small business, as it can be run by one or two key workers, allowing it to respond quickly to its customers' demands, etc.

Again, using examples will give you the best opportunity to show that you know and understand about business structures.

Learning outcome two – Marketing

PC (a) – Evaluation of the role and importance of marketing to business is accurate and makes reference to product and market orientation.

What you will be asked

This PC will ask you about three different things:

◆ about the role of marketing

◆ about the importance of marketing

◆ about product and market orientation.

Answer

Marketing is the method used by the business to communicate with the consumer. It allows them to find out what consumers are willing to buy, and at what price, and allows them to inform consumers about the organization and its products.

It is important as it will allow them to identify, anticipate and satisfy consumer's needs. This is essential if the business is to achieve its objectives.

In market orientation the business concentrates on finding out what consumers want and then providing that product or service, whereas product orientation is where the business concentrates on the product or the production process without researching what consumers' needs actually are.

Market orientated businesses are likely to be much more successful as they are more likely to achieve the sales level required to make profits. Product orientated businesses believe rely on product innovation and technical advancement to stimulate sales and achieve premium pricing.

PC (b) – Analysis of marketing decisions of an organization is accurate with respect to its marketing mix and target markets.

What you will be asked

Firstly you will be asked to identify examples of the elements of the marketing mix from the case study you are given. Secondly, you will be asked to explain what target markets are using undifferentiated and differentiated marketing, market segmentation and niche marketing. You will then be asked for examples form the case study.

Answer

A lot will depend on the case study you are given. There will be no marks given for identifying the 4 P's, what is needed is for you to show that you know what they are.

Use your textbook or notes to learn the definitions for undifferentiated and differentiated marketing, market segmentation and niche marketing, and then try to find examples of them in the case study.

PC (c) – Evaluation of the product mix of an organisation is accurate and makes reference to new product development and ways of prolonging the life of existing products.

What you will be asked

There are two parts here, firstly you will be asked about the product mix or product portfolio of the business and why it is important to have a range of products. Secondly you will be asked to describe extension strategies for the product life cycle.

Answer

Businesses benefit from having a range of products in their product mix as having products at different stages in the product life cycle means that as one product goes into decline another is ready to take its place in the growth or maturity stage. This allows the organisation to keep profits levels high, and products that are at maturity stage will give the business enough money to develop new products to replace them.

Hints and Tips

A well drawn product portfolio diagram may help you get full marks here!

Answer

Businesses may extend the life cycle of their products by introducing extension strategies such as a new advertising campaign; finding alternative markets or uses for the product; or restyling the product or its packaging.

Hints and Tips

Good examples would help get full marks here.

PC (d) – Analysis of reasons for market research is accurate and makes reference to market research techniques.

What you will be asked

You will be asked why market research is important and then asked to describe with examples different types of market research techniques.

> ### Answer
>
> Market research is important because it allows the organisation to find out about what is going on in their market, such as who their customers are, how much they will be willing to pay for products, and what they will want in the future. It also allows the them to find out what competitors are doing and allows them to test potential new products.

In the second part of the PC you may have to refer to the case study, but you should describe different field and desk research techniques and say why they might be used by specific businesses under different circumstance.

Learning Outcome three – Finance

There are three PC's for this assessment. The assessment will be based on a case study which you should read carefully before attempting to answer the questions as your answers will be based on the type of business in the case study.

PC (a) – Interpretation of cash flow information is accurate and related to possible cash flow problems.

What you will be asked

You will be given a cash flow statement and then asked to identify possible problems for the organisation involved, you then have to explain what this will mean for the organization, such as what they should do.

> ### Answer
>
> What you should write for an answer will depend very much on what case study you are given. However, there are a number of things to look out for.
>
> The most obvious indication of problems will appear in the closing cash balances if they become negative, or reduce over a period of months, then this will highlight where the problems exist.
>
> The first thing to look for is falling sales receipts. This could be due to seasonal factors or poor sales techniques. In either case if they are not matched by a fall in payments then there will be a problem.
>
> *Answer continued* ➤

Answer *continued*

Also, look out for big items of capital expenditure such as new machines.

The implications will be that the organisation will have to reduce some of their outflows of cash.

You will have to say which, and explain why. If there is a large item of capital expenditure then perhaps the organisation should have considered getting a loan and paying it off over a period of time, or perhaps they should now consider sale and leaseback in order to solve their cash flow problems.

PC (b) – Appropriate financial ratios are used correctly to interpret the performance and liquidity of a business.

What you will be asked
You will be given a set of ratios that have been calculated for you. You then have to decide which to use for performance and which one to use for liquidity.

Answer

The easy way to remember is that profitability ratios will be based on gross or net profit, whilst liquidity ratios will be concerned with current assets and current liabilities.

You will be expected to compare the ratios of two companies or two different years for the same company, and state which is better or worse and why.

For performance/profitability you could look at the cost of goods sold compared to the gross profit, this should show whether the business should look to increase selling price or look for cheaper suppliers. Either of these should increase profitability. However, increasing price can reduce sales, and cheaper suppliers may not be able to give you the quality or quantity of goods that you need. The difference between gross and net profit is the expenses the firm has had to pay during the year. If the net profit ratio reduces more that the gross profit then the business should look at ways of reducing expenses. In your answer you should give some examples such as reducing wages by laying-off non-essential workers.

The liquidity ratios compare current assets and current liabilities. Current assets are in the form of cash (eg cash at bank) or in a form that can readily be turned into cash such as debtors. Current liabilities are bills that the business will have to pay in the very near future.

Whichever of the liquidity ratios you decide to use, the important thing to remember is that if the business cannot raise enough money to pay its bills it will be in serious trouble.

Answer *continued* ➤

Answer *continued*

So if the ratio is too low then the business will have to find cash quickly. This can be done in a variety of ways and your answer will depend on the business in the case study. However, selling off unwanted assets or stock, sale and leaseback, getting a bank loan, or selling shares may be appropriate. On the other hand if the ratio is too high it means that the business has money lying around and should invest it in the bank or in new capital.

PC (c) – Explanation of budgets is accurate and refers to their role in monitoring and controlling business activities.

Remember that we are talking about all types of budgets here not just cash budgets.

What you will be asked
You will be asked to explain what budgets are and how management can use them to help ensure that the business achieves its objectives.

Answer

Budgets are plans for the future usually expressed in financial terms. All sections of the business will be given a budget in terms of how they are expected to perform in the months or year ahead.

Budgets allow managers to plan for the future; they help set targets for managers, making them accountable for their decisions; they can be used to compare actual performance to the budgeted performance and take appropriate action where necessary; and see how they are progressing towards their objectives.

Learning outcome four – Human Resource Management

PC (a) – Explanation of the main stages in the recruitment process is accurate and related to the requirements of a business enterprise.

What you will be asked
What you will actually be asked will depend on the case study that you are given by your teacher/lecturer, however, it will cover the 3 stages of Job Analysis, Job Description, and Person Specification.

Answer

Job analysis is a study of what tasks are involved in the job, what skills and level of performance is required. It will highlight whether or not a vacancy actually exists.

Job Description is a description of what tasks are required to be completed within the job, and what level of experience, qualifications, and skills will be required. The job description may well be used for preparing the job advert.

Person specification is the profile of the person you actually want to do the job. It would look at the personality and other skills you would wish the job holder to have. It can then be compared with applications to find the best matches.

What you will be asked
The second part of this PC deals with internal and external sources of recruitment.

Answer

Internal sources are recruitment from within the organisation. These employees will already be known to the organisation and so there should be a greater chance of them being suitable for the job. Promotion prospects will increase motivation among staff, and will make it easier to recruit from outside the organisation. It is quicker and cheaper than external recruitment.

External sources give a much wider choice of candidates, and you can gain new skills currently not available within the existing workforce. Useful when introducing new types of products or new technology to the organisation as it will reduce the cost of training existing staff. External recruitment also brings new ideas to the organisation.

PC (b) – Evaluation of the selection process is accurate and makes reference to selection methods and their effectiveness in securing a suitable appointment for a business enterprise.

What you will be asked
This PC will ask you about the effectiveness of selection and again is in two parts. The first is to identify methods of selecting applicants.

Answer

Application forms which allow all applicants to answer the same questions, and so are easier to compare. These can be matched to the person specification so that suitable candidates can be more easily identified.

Interviews allow a meeting face to face with the candidates, where further questions can be asked of the applicants, and they also have the opportunity to ask questions. Interviewers should try to focus on the information rather than personal feeling about the applicant. The interviews should be fair to all applicants and give them the best opportunity to show why they should be given the job.

References should be sought from previous employers/schools/etc. They are useful to check that the information contained in the application form is correct, and will give further information on the person's character.

Testing will allow the organisation to find out more about the applicant's aptitude and personality, including their ability to problem solve and their most suitable role in team-work etc.

What you will be asked
The second part asks why an effective recruitment process is so important.

Answer

An effective process will ensure that the correct applicant is selected. This will avoid the need to go through the process again, reduce staff turnover, and the need for additional training. It will give the applicant the opportunity to find out if they really want to work for the organisation.

PC (c) – Analysis of employee relations in a business organization is accurate and makes reference to employee representation.

What you will be asked
This PC focuses on the importance of employee relations. Again there are 2 parts. The first is on the importance of employee relations to the organisation.

Answer

Good employee relations helps to increase cooperation of the workforce to enable the organisation to meet its objectives, helping to motivate the workforce and improve communication between staff and management, and to allow for the inclusion of employees in decision-making.

What you will be asked
The second part is on the forms of employee representation.

Answer

Works councils are regular meetings of representatives of employees and management to discuss issues that affect employees. The representatives have a statutory right to access information.

Trade Unions will have agreements in place with the employers and will meet to discuss issues of importance to the employees.

Staff meetings could be arranged to discuss matters of concern to both employees and management, or to carry out consultation.

PC (d) – Reference to current legislative requirements affecting the management of human resources in business enterprises are accurate.

What you will be asked
The question will ask you to give examples of current legislation that human resources departments will need to worry about.

Answer

You will simply have to write about a number of different pieces of legislation. You don't have to remember all the dates but you should give the correct names. (For example, it is the Health and Safety at Work Act, not the Health and Safety Act).

You should then go on to explain what the implications for the firm are due to these pieces of legislation.

Learning outcome five – Operations Management

PC (a) – Analysis of the importance of purchasing to a business is accurate and makes reference to factors which influence purchasing decisions.

What you will be asked
What you are asked to do here will depend on which assessment you are given, and you should always try to use examples from the case study. This assessment has two parts and the first is on the importance of purchasing.

Answer

The materials that the business purchases will affect the quality of the final product so the organisation must make sure that it gets the right quantities of materials at the right price and of the right quality, at the right time.

Good purchasing can reduce the cost of production and so increase profitability, and make sure that the final products are what the customer wants, so reducing returns and complaints.

What you will be asked
The second part is about the factors that influence purchasing decisions.

Answer

What quantity to purchase will depend on how much suitable storage space is available. It will also be influenced by what discount the business can get for bulk buying, and the cost of holding stock.

Other factors the business will have to consider include Are the suppliers reliable? Can they guarantee quality?

PC (b) – Analysis of factors affecting the quality of operations of an organisation is accurate with respect to organisational and customer requirements.

What you will be asked
This PC also has three parts. The first is why should the organisation be worried about what the customer wants in terms of quality?

Answer

Customers can go elsewhere if they are not happy, and having quality procedures will make sure that customers will receive what the organisation say they will get.

Quality standards may encourage continuous improvement in the organisation's production, and that with high quality products they may be able to target different market segments.

What you will be asked

The second part is about how quality standards can help the business meet its own objectives.

Answer

The organisation has to provide products at the quality standards that they say they are going to, and that this would mean making available the resources needed to achieve that level of quality.

The organisation's requirements must be at least of the same quality level as customers would expect from their product.

What you will be asked

The third part of the PC deals with the methods available to ensure quality operations.

Answer

Quality Control – checking the final product for faults.

Benchmarking comparing the organisation against the best in the industry and setting standards to match the best.

TQM – where the organisation has quality chains established with every member of the organisation responsible for quality, and where quality is checked at every stage.

Quality Circles – where groups of workers meet to solve production problems and try to find ways of improving the process.

PC (c) – Analysis of different types of production is accurate to the product or services provided.

What you will be asked

This PC is split into two parts. The first is about giving suitable examples of where Job, Batch, and Flow production are used. It may be based on the case study you are given, or you may be asked to give your own examples.

Answer

This depends very much on the assessment you are given, sorry! Make sure you know of examples of each.

What you will be asked

The second part asks you to show you understand what each type of production is.

> ## Answer
>
> **Job production** is for on-off jobs, usually to the customer's individual requirements.
>
> **Batch production** is where products are produced in batches because demand for the product will vary but will be too much for job production.
>
> **Flow production** is used where there is continuous demand for the product, and economies of scale are available from mass production.

CASE STUDY AND PRACTICE EXAMINATION QUESTIONS

Case Study – 'Mikes'

The following case study and questions are very similar to what you will see if the final exam. The problems in the case study are easier to find than in a real case study in the exam, however, this will help you to build up the techniques that you will need for the real exam.

Change at the Firm

Derek and Susan Thomson are a husband and wife team who own and run the Mike's sandwich chain. They bought the business three years ago; they'd previously been franchisees of a rival sandwich chain, but having got to know the industry, they wanted to be in total control of their own operation.

A venture capital company helped them raise the £20 million needed to buy Mike's and they established a new management team to run the company and initiate a series of radical changes.

"What we tried to do was bring the business under one identity, so people would know what we stand for, which is value, quality and variety," says Susan.

Mike's

Mike's had been established in 1989 producing cheap products at low prices; it was profitable and had potential to grow, but there were problems.

The Head Office consisted of just three people, with no infrastructure or control over the business, so management was poor. There was no unified Mike's identity, and an out-dated system of dealing with suppliers.

The shops were dull with a limited product range; some stores made their own sandwiches and Health and Safety rules were scarcely met.

Market research

After commissioning a research programme to understand what consumers wanted, in 2001 they began an aggressive advertising campaign, with a new logo and a new look for the stores, and the range of products on offer was expanded.

The number of stores has now grown from 32 to 57 with plans to open a further 30 in the rest of the UK. But perhaps the most dramatic changes the Thomsons brought about was to their core business; food manufacturing.

The factory they bought was run by a small under-skilled team with low staff moral, making it a low quality facility. It required massive investment to turn it into a state of the art operation, with an efficient in-house delivery system.

Many of the shops were producing on their own site where the quality of the product was unreliable, and were reluctant to make the move to central production.

Solutions

The management team was strengthened with food industry specialists and over £1 250 000 was spent improving the fabric, layout and capacity of the site.

By the end of May 2002 the final phase of factory development was completed giving the site the capacity to service almost double the number of stores that it does at the present time. Each week 40 000 loaves of bread and two tonnes of tuna is delivered into the factory and turned into sandwiches for the company's stores. Production has rocketed from 10 000 items per day to 75 000.

Keeping a tight control on costs is seen as vital for the success of the business, so that they can charge the prices they do and still make profit.

The Future

The Thomson's plan was to turn a small-player in the sandwich shop industry into one of the country's leading food brands, and this year the firm has announced record profits of £3 million and a new £4 million expansion plan.

Section One Questions

1   Identify the problems that Mike's faced when taken over by the Thomsons. Use the following headings to construct your answer.

   ◆   Marketing

   ◆   Finance

   ◆   Operations

   ◆   Other   *(10 Marks)*

2   The Thomsons originally ran a franchise for a rival sandwich firm. Describe the advantages and disadvantages of franchising to:

   (i) The Franchisee

   (ii) The Franchisor

   (8 Marks)

3   (a)   The Thomsons raised long term
finance for their business with the
help of venture capital company.

Describe an advantage and a
disadvantage for 2 other sources of
finance which the company could
use.   (4 Marks)

(b)   How might the borrowing affect an
organisations cash flow:

(i)   in the short run

(ii)   in the long run?   (2 Marks)

4   A research programme was carried out
by the Thomsons to understand what
consumers wanted.

(a)   Describe two methods of market research and explain the advantages and
disadvantages of each.   (6 Marks)

(b)   The market research would be used to make decisions for the improvement
of the business. What methods can the owners of the business use to ensure
that their decisions are the correct ones?   (8 Marks)

(c)   How could the business assess the effectiveness of the decisions that it has
made.   (1 Marks)

5   Many firms now outsource part of their production. For example, Thomsons
could outsource their sandwich production.

Describe the advantages and disadvantages of outsourcing for an
organisation.   (8 Marks)

Section Two Questions

1   High street banks in the UK have been criticised for making very high profits
from their customers. They will want to show that they still offer very good
services to the public.

a)   Describe the role of the public relations officer in achieving this
objective.   (4 marks)

b)   Why do some firms spend vast sums of money on product
innovation?   (3 marks)

c)   What measures can an organisation take to try to make sure that their new
product is a success?   (8 marks)

d)   Many firms now operate in a global market. Discuss how modern
information and communication technology can be used to communicate
and trade globally.   (6 marks)

e)   Describe the problems that can occur when using modern technology.
(4 marks)

2 Many organisations go to great lengths to develop a corporate culture.

a) Explain why this might be important and what factors can be influenced. *(6 marks)*

b) Describe the actions an organisation should take when changing from a tall to a flat structure to ensure that the change is a success. *(5 marks)*

c) How could the organisation measure the effectiveness of such a change? *(4 marks)*

d) Describe the various employment law issues that must be considered when change takes place in an organisation. *(10 marks)*

3 Many firms are looking at the new business opportunities available from the enlargement of the European Union.

a) Describe the benefits and drawbacks of using a structured decision-making model when deciding to try to take advantage of these new opportunities. *(7 marks)*

b) Discuss the characteristics of good quality information that would lead to good decisions being made. *(6 marks)*

c) Identify and describe the objectives that a marketing department will have for the new markets that will be open to the business. *(5 marks)*

d) Describe the influence governments abroad may have on the business' marketing campaign. *(5 marks)*

e) Why are demographics important to the business? *(2 marks)*

4 BT and Yahoo joined together to provide a new ISP service for ordinary modem and broadband customers.

a) Identify and describe the type of integration that this partnership represents. *(2 marks)*

b) The Internet market is still in the growth stage, whilst the mobile phone market is at the saturation stage. Compare the characteristics of each of these stages in the product life cycle. *(6 marks)*

c) Describe the effects on an organisation's cash flow of each of these stages.
   (4 marks)

d) The balance sheet gives a financial overview of a business at a particular point in time. Describe each of the main headings in the balance sheet.
   (8 marks)

e) Staff appraisal is seen as a method of increasing the effectiveness of an organisation. Describe the main objectives of a staff appraisal programme.
   (5 marks)

Section One Answers

1   Marketing

No unified Mike's identity

Quality of product is unreliable

Shops were dull

Limited product range

Cheap products at low prices

Finance

Venture Capitalists will want a share of the profits/may not agree to re-investment.

They could also take over the business and force the owners out.

Need to raise finance for the planned expansion.

Low prices mean low profit margins – if there are increases in raw material costs or running costs it could be difficult to maintain profit margins.

Operations

Products varied in quality.

Some stores made their own sandwiches (explained).

Out of date system of dealing with suppliers.

Many shops producing on site and were reluctant to move to a central location.

Health and safety rules were scarcely met.

Other

Head Office consisted of just 3 people.

No infrastructure or control over the business.

Hints and Tips

There are a maximum of 3 marks under each of the headings. The answers must appear under the correct headings to get the marks.

2 a) **Advantages**

- The franchisee is usually getting a proven business success.
- The new business gets the existing well established name.
- It will be helped and supported by the franchiser.
- It is easier to borrow to buy a franchise than to develop an untried idea.

Disadvantages

- The business has to be run in the way the franchiser wants it to be.
- If the franchiser goes out of business or sells the chain to another company, the franchisee's business may be at risk.
- The franchisee will probably have to pay a regular fee to the franchiser.
- The payment may be a percentage of the profits, in which case the more successful the franchisee is, the more it will have to pay.

b) **Advantages**

- The franchiser can expand its business without having to open more branches, or train and recruit more staff.
- Many of the risks are taken on by the franchisee.
- The franchisee will work hard and be highly motivated.

Disadvantages

- The franchiser's reputation depends on how good the franchisees are.
- One piece of bad publicity can affect the whole business.
- Some control over the business can be lost.

Hints and Tips

When allocating marks, the examiner will restrict the number of marks available for each part of the question. For example, in this question, a maximum of six marks per section may be allowed. Both advantages and disadvantages will be required for full marks.

3 a)
- (Bank) loan: The company can receive a large sum straight away and pay it back over a period of time to suit the business. Loans are easy to obtain.
- Mortgage: These have the same advantages as a loan, and they usually attract a lower rate of interest.

◆ Debentures: These have a fixed rate of interest. Large sums can be raised.

◆ Share issue: Large sums can be raised, and it is not necessary to pay them back.

◆ Grant: A grant does not have to be replied.

Hints and *Tips*

One mark will be given for identifying a source, and one for an advantage.

b) ◆ In the short term, more cash is available for the business.

◆ In the long term, the money may have to be repaid, or more higher dividends may have to be paid.

4 a) **Primary research**

◆ This is gathered by the organisation for its own purposes.

◆ It is more accurate, up-to-date and relevant.

◆ It is costly to collect.

◆ It is time-consuming to analyse the data.

Secondary/desk research

◆ This is gathered by someone else for their own purposes, but it can be reused.

◆ It is much cheaper.

◆ It is readily available.

◆ It may be inaccurate or out-of-date.

Hints and *Tips*

The examiners will give credit for examples (for instance 'questionnaire') if they are correctly described. The marks will be restricted to a maximum of approximately four marks for each type of research.

b)

Hints and *Tips*

The examiners will give one mark for each step in the structured decision-making model, but a maximum of only half the marks for a simple list.

- Identify the problem: Set the aims.
- Identify the objectives: What is it that we want to achieve?
- Gather information: Good information leads to good decision-making. Extensive use of internal and external information is required.
- Analyse information: Study the information collected. What can you do, and what can you not do? What will help, and what will not?
- Devise various solutions: Decide on a number of courses of action that could be taken that would meet the aims.
- Select from various solutions: Select the one that will be most likely to meet the aims of the organisation.
- Communicate the decision: If everybody knows what they are doing and why, they will be far more motivated to succeed.
- Implement the decision: Arrange for the resources to be put into place.
- Evaluate: Using the information that is being collected on how the process is going, compare this with what was expected to happen.

Hints *and* Tips

Marks would also be available for answers mentioning SWOT analysis.

c)

- To monitor and control the business, the management would compare the situation before and after for changes in demand, profitability and production. [One mark would be given for each if they were explained.]

Hints *and* Tips

This type of question often causes problems. You have to use your common sense.

- The business could carry out further market research.
- It could do a SWOT analysis. [Watch out for repetition.]

5 **Advantages**

- The specialist firm may be able to carry out the function at a lower cost.
- It allows for more precise matching of supply to demand.

- The organisation does not have to buy expensive equipment that may not be efficiently used.
- The organisation can concentrate on its areas of strength.
- By using outside suppliers, firms have the opportunity to redesign their operations to make use of the expertise of suppliers.
- A just-in-time system could be used.

Disadvantages

- The organisation can lose control over quality.
- It is less able to monitor the work being done.
- The organisation loses some expertise and experience in the areas being outsourced, which may provide a competitive advantage.
- It loses some control over delivery dates.
- It loses influence over the reduction of costs.
- Some profits may go to the specialist firm.
- Some activities are confidential and should be kept within the organisation.

> **Hints and Tips**
>
> The marks would be restricted to a maximum of five or six if only advantages were mentioned or if only disadvantages were mentioned.

Section Two Answers

1 a)
- Organises press releases.
- Arranges press conferences with free products for those who attend.
- Organises public relations activities.
- Responds to criticism in a manner that shows the banks in a good light.
- Arranges for donations to charities.
- Organises and highlights any corporate responsibility activities.
- Arranges sponsorship.

Hints and Tips

Only four marks are available, so you will only have to mention four points. However, you will need to expand on these points slightly. For example, for the first point you could write the following.

'the public relations officer will arrange to issue press releases detailing how the profits were made, and stating that high profits are only made in well run businesses.'

b) ◆ There are high rewards for being the market leader in terms of profits and market share.

◆ The firm wants to stay ahead of its competitors.

◆ The firm wants to extend/ increase its market share.

Hints and Tips

Only three marks are available, so three points will do, or possibly four for safety.

◆ It boosts the image of the business.

◆ The business needs to replace products that have gone into decline.

c) ◆ Carry out market research to find out what consumers want.

◆ Decide whether or not it is possible to make the product.

◆ Produce a prototype to see what it would look like.

◆ Ask consumers what they think of the product.

◆ Adapt the product as necessary.

◆ Launch the product into a test market, and adapt it again if necessary.

◆ Put finance in place.

◆ Decide on a price.

◆ Obtain patents, trademarks, etc.

◆ Advertise the new product.

◆ Launch the product in the whole market.

Only six marks are available, but there is a great deal you could write about. Do not be tempted to spend a lot of time answering this question just because you know a lot about it. You can either pick three types of technology and make two points about each, or pick six and make one point about each.

d)

You could choose any of the following.

- Internet.
- E-mail.
- Mobile phones and WAP technology.
- Wireless technology.
- Videoconferencing.
- Fax.
- Satellite links.

You should write about what each can do and how that helps businesses communicate globally. For example you could write the following.

'The Internet allows 24 hour a day communication. Text and graphics, spreadsheet and database information can be sent instantly. You can use passwords for security.'

e)
- Technology can fail, with the loss of important data.
- Viruses can destroy information and prevent communication.
- Technology needs to be updated, which often involves staff training.
- The costs of updating hardware and software can be high, as can the costs of training.
- Technology can be abused by staff (for instance via the Internet and e-mail).

2 a) Corporate culture is important because it influences how staff behave and deal with customers.
- It can affect their attitude to work.
- It can affect their level of motivation.
- It can influence how workers act in relation to the businesses objectives.
- It can influence how staff communicate internally and externally.
- It can allow new members of staff to fit in quickly.

There are two parts to this question. First you are asked why corporate culture is important. This is probably worth only one or two marks, so do not spend too much time on it. The second part of the question is about what the corporate culture can influence, and most of the marks will be available for this.

b)
- Make sure that all the staff are aware of the reasons for change, and what new duties they will be expected to perform.
- Arrange any training that is needed.
- Empower workers to allow them to make decisions.
- Make sure the span of control is suitable for staff.
- Put additional resources in place where needed.
- Monitor and evaluate each stage of the change.

c)
- Ask staff if they feel the changes are working.
- Compare production before and after the change. Look at number of faults and areas of waste.
- Compare sales or levels of customer satisfaction before and after.
- Compare staff absences before and after.

Hints and Tips

This might seem like a hard question for four marks. However, the business will have to be careful that the changes do not change any of the policies that were in place before, so you can write about any of the areas.

d)
- The organisation must ensure that the new structure allows for equal pay regardless of sex (Equal Pay Act 1970).
- It must make sure that those who are demoted or made redundant do not have a claim on the basis of sex discrimination, either directly or indirectly. All men and women must be treated equally (Sex Discrimination Act 1975).
- It must make sure that the organisation has not discriminated against any of the staff, either directly or indirectly (Race Relations Act 1976).
- It must make sure that anyone who is to be made redundant is given the statutory notice, and is given redundancy payments if he or she is entitled to them.
- The new operation has to comply with the Working Time Regulations 1998, so that the staff do not have to work longer hours than are lawful under the new structure.

◆ The staff cannot be put under undue stress owing to the additional workload placed on them.

◆ All health and safety regulations must be met.

Hints and Tips

There is a lot more that you could write. However, only ten marks are available, so you should try to make at least ten points but not more than 12.

3   a)   **Benefits**

◆ The time taken to use the model means that the decision is thought through, and is more likely to be the correct one.

◆ The decision is based on the fullest and highest-quality information available, so it is more likely to be the right one.

◆ The creation of alternatives allows you to develop the other options fully should the first decision not work as expected.

Drawbacks

◆ Using the model takes a long time, so if the decision has to be made quickly, the model will not be of any use.

◆ It is not always possible to gather all the information needed. Collecting the information may prove to be too expensive to be worthwhile.

◆ It may not be possible to come up with good alternatives.

◆ The model does not allow for the creativity of managers, who may feel they already know what to do.

◆ Managers may not be able to come up with any creative solutions.

Hints and Tips

The question asks for both benefits and drawbacks, so you will need to include both. You will probably only receive a maximum of four points if you do not include both.

b)

◆ Accurate: There should be no errors.

◆ Timely: It has to be up-to-date and available when needed.

◆ Complete: All the information needed should be there.

◆ Appropriate: It should be relevant to the problem.

◆ Available: It has to be easily obtainable.

◆ Economical: It has to be cost-effective, and not too expensive.

◆ Objective: It should be free from bias.

◆ Concise: It has to be able to be summarised into easily readable relevant information.

c) ◆ To increase sales revenue and profitability.

◆ To increase market share.

◆ To maintain or improve the image of the business, its brand or its products.

◆ To target the new market for sales.

◆ To develop new and improved products.

d) ◆ They will decide if the products are safe, or require additional features.

◆ They will decide what is an acceptable advertisement.

◆ They may add local tax that will increase the price of the product.

◆ They may have existing laws on maximum prices.

◆ They may have restrictions on when advertisements for certain products may be shown on television.

e) Demographics is the study of the structure of the population in terms of age, gender, household income, buying patterns and lifestyle. It is important because it helps the organisation to identify its customers, and focus its marketing strategies more directly.

Hints and Tips

One mark is available for the definition of demographics, even though this was not asked for. Identification marks are few, but it does not do any harm to give a brief description.

4 a) This is vertical integration. and Yahoo operate different stages in the production of internet services.

b) ◆ At the growth stage, the number of customers is still increasing, whereas at the saturation stage, the number of customers has reached its maximum unless action is taken.

◆ During the growth stage, businesses may not achieve profitability. However, at the saturation stage, the profits are at their highest level.

◆ Advertising during the growth stage is aimed at convincing customers to use the Internet, whereas at the saturation stage, advertising is used to take customers from rival businesses.

c) During the growth stage, the flow of money into the business is less than at saturation. More money is spent on advertising during the growth stage, so there is a possibility that more money will be going out than coming in. Loans and overdrafts need to be arranged where necessary at the growth stage, while during saturation, the business will be clearing its debts or receiving large amounts of cash that should be invested.

d) ◆ **Fixed assets**: These are the assets that the business means to keep in order to continue trading. They are usually high-value. They are shown at net book value after any depreciation or revaluation. Examples are machines, delivery vehicles, and buildings.

◆ **Current assets**: These are the assets that the business has either in the form of money, or which are to be changed into money, such as stock, debtors, and cash at the bank.

◆ **Current liabilities**: These are sums of money that the business will have to pay in the near future. They include payments to suppliers, wages still to be paid, and dividends still to be paid.

◆ **Financed by**: This shows where the money for the business has come from and any reserves the business has. It includes the various types of share in the business, debentures, and long-term borrowing.

e) ◆ To identify future training needs.

◆ To consider development needs for the individual's career.

◆ To improve the performance of the employee.

◆ To provide feedback to the employee about his or her performance.

◆ To identify staff members who have the potential for future promotion, or who have additional skills that could be useful now or in the future.